Best
TEA SHOP WALKS
in
SNOWDONIA

Dorothy Hamilton

Published by Sigma Leisure – an imprint of
Sigma Press, 1 South Oak Lane, Wilmslow, Cheshire SK9 6AR, England.

British Library Cataloguing in Publication Data
A CIP record for this book is available from the British Library.

ISBN: 1-85058-686-1

Typesetting and Design by: Sigma Press, Wilmslow, Cheshire.

Cover: The Mawddach Estuary (Nick Lambert)

Maps and photographs: The author

Printed by: MFP Design and Print

Disclaimer: the information in this book is given in good faith and is believed to be correct at the time of publication. No responsibility is accepted by either the author or publisher for errors or omissions, or for any loss or injury howsoever caused. Only you can judge your own fitness, competence and experience.

Contents

The Walks

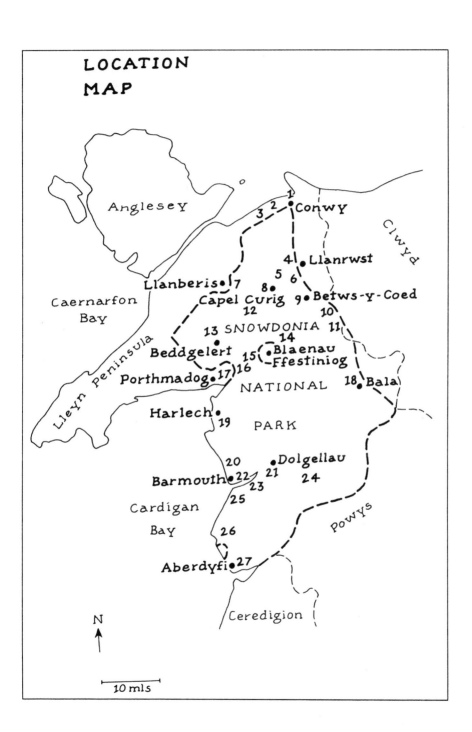

Introduction to Snowdonia

Snowdonia National Park offers an immense variety of scenery from high mountains, moorland and wooded river gorges to green valleys, estuaries and coastline. Miles of footpaths traversing the area permit superb walking through magnificent landscape.

The massive breaks in the mountains, running north to south in Snowdonia, were created when Cambrian and later rocks were forced against the harder pre-Cambrian rocks of Anglesey during the extensive earth movements which uplifted North Wales above the sea. Earlier volcanic activity under the sea had caused igneous rocks to be pushed through the sedimentary layers. When these layers wore away they left behind Snowdonia's mountains. The 600 million years old Cambrian rocks, the oldest rocks in Snowdonia, are exposed in the Rhinog mountains, which lie parallel to the coast east of Harlech.

The Ice Age began about 80,000 years ago and for the next 70,000 years, apart from mild periods, Snowdonia was covered in ice. The glaciers moved slowly to sea level, grinding away rock to form amphitheatres in the mountains, and smoothing stream-shaped 'V' valleys into 'U' shapes. Nearly all the lakes in the National Park are of glacial origin. Some have been dammed by moraines whilst others were scooped out by glaciers.

When the last of the glaciers disappeared, wind, rain, snow and frost continued to wear away the rock, creating soil. Rivers and streams carried this soil to lower slopes and valleys enabling plants to grow. In the warmer drier climate woodlands flourished. Birches and sessile oaks clothed valleys and lower mountain slopes. Some remnants of the deciduous woodlands remain, especially in the Vale of Ffestiniog.

Nowadays a few flowers grow in the high mountains. These include purple mountain saxifrage, moss campion, mountain avens and, in inaccessible places, the rare Snowdon lily. On almost any walk a buzzard will soar overhead. Peregrines nest in the national park. The deep croak of the raven is a familiar sound in the mountain environment whilst the red beak and legs of the rare chough may be spotted in areas close to old quarries. On the high rocks, wrens are more frequently seen than the shy ring ouzel.

On the lower slopes, wheatears and meadow pipits flit between boulders while skylarks spiral overhead. Herons may be seen in damper places looking for fish and frogs in streams. The herds of goats are descendants of once domesticated animals. Foxes may be spotted on heather hillsides and occasionally a stoat or polecat. Bell heather is the first heather to flower, followed by ling (Scottish heather) and the cross-leafed heath. The insect-eating sundew grows in damp places. Water lilies are found on many lakes.

At all times of the year there are birds in the estuaries. Plovers, lapwing, oystercatcher, dunlins and sanderling trot along the water's edge. At Porthmadog there is a large community of swans.

Plenty of birds are to be found in the sessile oaklands. Look for nuthatches, tree creepers, woodpeckers, jays, redstarts, finches, tits and pied flycatchers. In the river gorges there will be dippers and grey wagtails skipping amongst the boulders. Numerous grey squirrels run along the branches. Wood anemone, sorrel, wood avens, primrose, bluebell and violet carpet the woodland floor in early spring. The fast growing coniferous plantations attract fewer birds but there is a possibility of seeing goldcrest, siskin and redpoll. Polecat and the rare pine marten are found in the Gwydr Forest whilst deer graze in Coed y Brenin.

The earliest visible remains of man in Snowdonia are the Neolithic burial chambers. It was during this era that people started to practise agriculture, cutting down some of the primeval woodland. Stone circles belong to the later Bronze Age and the Druid's Circle above Penmaenmawr is a fine example. It has been famous since horse-drawn coaches crossed the Carneddau mountains.

Celtic-speaking people came to Wales during the Iron Age establishing innumerable forts on the hilltops. There is a hillfort on the ridge of Conwy Mountain. Founded in AD77 by Agricola, Segontium in Caernarfon was the main Roman fort in North Wales and it was garrisoned until the end of the 4th century. Some sections of Roman road can still be walked in the Carneddau mountains, south of Betws y Coed and east of Trawsfynydd.

During the following centuries, whilst Danes and Saxons invaded and settled in England, the struggles in Wales were mainly between rival overlords. At the beginning of the 13th century, Llywelyn ap Iorwerth (the Great) emerged as a strong ruler. He constructed stone castles at Dolwyddelan, Dolbadarn (Llanberis), Criccieth and Castell y Bere. Disputes of inheritance followed his death but his grandson Llywelyn ap Gruffudd (the Last) was recognised as Prince of Wales by Henry III. However, Llywelyn refused homage to Henry's successor, his son Edward I. Llywelyn's brother Dafydd made more trouble by provoking Edward into war and Llywelyn was killed near Builth Wells in Mid Wales. Later, Dafydd was caught and executed. This was the end of Welsh independence. Edward I consolidated his victory by building a chain of castles at Conwy, Caernarfon, Beaumaris and Harlech. His eldest son was made the Prince of Wales.

By the 13th century Snowdonia had lost much of its forest to shipbuilding, housing and clearing land for cattle and crops. The nibbling of sheep and goats prevented the regrowth of trees. Cattle and sheep were taken in great droves to markets in England, some as far as Smithfield. Most of their routes are now metalled roads but their grassy tracks remain in the Rhinog range.

In the 19th century the slate industry not only drastically changed the landscape in certain areas, it also brought about a shipbuilding boom. In comparison, the small copper, lead and gold mines have made little impact on the countryside. The majority of the slate quarries are on the fringes of the national park, but many present day visitors find industrial heritage to be an interesting aspect to this historic corner of Wales.

The Tea Shops

By ending your walk at a tea room, you experience the best combination of a day out in Wales – a ramble through Snowdonia's beautiful countryside followed by an appetising light meal.

Apart from Welsh cream teas, many of the teashops have Welsh specialities such as bara brith. This is a yeast fruit bread, sometimes made with wholemeal flour. Welsh cakes are a kind of griddle cake containing dried fruit. Most tea rooms offer a variety of home-made fare, especially home baking.

Whether a remote farmhouse, a village post office or a luxurious town tea room, all the tea shops welcome walkers, but please be considerate and remove muddy boots. The establishments themselves are varied and several offer something other than refreshments. Some may be attached to woollen mills, narrow gauge railways, book shops or small museums. Many are in buildings hundreds of years old and two are in former courtrooms.

Some of the tea shops are only open in the summer months and

others may close for a short period in the winter. If walking early or
late in the year it is advisable to check opening hours. The majority
of tea rooms would appreciate a telephone call in advance of a large
walking group.

The Walks

All the walks in this guide are circular. Ranging from 3½ to 8 miles,
they are suitable for families and all people of average fitness. A few
follow almost level paths but most require a little climbing. High
mountain routes are not included.

The walks offer plenty of variety – from woodland, forest and valley paths to high lakes and moorland. Some start at inland towns
and villages, others on the coast. They cover all of Snowdonia and
some walks start on the fringes of the National Park.

Walking boots are not essential for all the walks, but they are rec-
ommended for their ankle support and protection on rocky or
muddy paths. Warm clothing including head covering and gloves
are essential in the winter. Waterproofs should be carried if there is
any chance of rain. Drinks, hot or cold according to season, add en-
joyment to the longer walks.

The directions and maps in this guide book should be all you need
to find the way. However, carrying Ordnance Survey maps will help
you identify features in the surrounding countryside. The Ordnance
Survey maps referred to are the 1998 editions of the Outdoor Leisure
Series (2½ inches to 1mile), No's 17,18 and 23. The three cover all of
Snowdonia.

Public Transport

Nearly all the walks are accessible by public transport. Traffic in
some areas of Snowdonia is becoming a problem and you are urged
to use public transport in preference to travelling by car whenever
possible. Details are given for each walk. Free timetables are available from tourist information centres.

Welsh Place Names

Welsh is spoken as a first language in Snowdonia, especially away
from the coast. Everyone understands English but place names may
cause some difficulty. Learning these pronunciations will help.

```
 A  =  ah
 C  =  k (hard)
Dd  =  'th' as in 'the'
 E  =  eh
 F  =  v
Ff  =  f
 G  =  as in 'go'
 I  =  ee
Ll  =  say 'l', hold tongue in this position and blow gently
 O  =  oh
Th  =  as in through
 W  =  usually as in oo ('cwm' sounds like 'coom')
 Y  =  as e in 'the'
```

A few translations will aid understanding of place names. The following words are used frequently:

```
     Aber  =  estuary, river mouth
     Afon  =  river
     Allt  =  slope
Bach/fach  =  small
     Bedd  =  grave
    Betws  =  chapel
    Blaen  =  head of the valley
    Brith  =  speckled
     Bryn  =  hill
    Bwlch  =  pass
   Cadair  =  chair
      Cae  =  field
     Caer  =  fort
    Capel  =  chapel
  Castell  =  castle
     Cefn  =  ridge
  Ceunant  =  gorge
  Clogwyn  =  precipice
     Coch  =  red
     Coed  =  wood
    Craig  =  crag
    Croes  =  cross
      Cwm  =  valley
    Dinas  =  fort
 Dol/ddol  =  meadow
      Dwr  =  water
  Dyffryn  =  valley
   Eglwys  =  church
   Ffordd  =  road
   Ffridd  =  mountain pasture
  Ffynnon  =  well, spring
     Glan  =  river bank
```

Glas = blue, green
Gwyn = white
Hafod = summer dwelling
Hen = old
Hendre = winter dwelling
Isaf = lower
Llan = church
Llyn = lake
Maen = stone
Maes = field
Mawr/fawr = big
Melin/felin = mill
Moel/foel = hill
Morfa = marsh
Mynydd = mountain
Nant = stream
Newydd = new
Ogof = cave
Pant = hollow
Pen = head/top
Pentre = village
Plas = mansion
Pont/bont = bridge
Porth = port
Pwll = pool
Rhaeadr = waterfall
Rhiw = hill
Rhos = moorland
Rhyd = ford
Tan = under
Traeth = beach
Tref = town
Trwyn = promontory
Ty = house
Tyddyn = small farm
Uchaf = upper
Yn = in
Ynys = island

1. Conwy

Route: An easy footpath beside the estuary is followed by a steep climb to the ridge of Conwy Mountain. Throughout most of the walk there are spectacular views.

Distance: 6½ miles.

How to get there: From Bangor or Colwyn Bay take the A55 and then the A547.

Public Transport: Some trains on the Chester-Holyhead line stop at Conwy. Buses from Bangor and Llandudno.

Start: Conwy Harbour. Park in one of the signposted car parks.

Maps: Outdoor Leisure 17

Conwy is a charming, interesting old town guarded by a medieval castle and town walls. The thirteenth century castle, one of a string built by Edward I, stands high above the Conwy estuary. Designed by architect Master James of St George, it took four and a half years to build. Edward I spent Christmas here in 1294. During the Owain Glyndwr revolt, Welsh rebels captured Conwy on Good Friday 1401 and held the fortress for two months. The castle saw some action again in the Civil War and afterwards all fortifications were ordered to be made unusable. Fortunately little destruction took place and during the 19th century the castle became a tourist attraction.

The town walls are largely intact and it is possible to walk short sections along the top. The whole circuit is about 1300 metres with twenty-one towers. They were built the same time as the castle. Approaching the town from the east there is a good view of Thomas Telford's suspension bridge across afon Conwy. It was completed in 1826 and twenty years later Robert Stephenson opened his railway bridge nearby.

The Tea Shop

Anna's Tea Room is above the Conwy Outdoor Shop. Walk through the shop and climb the stairs to the Victorian tea room. The extensive menu includes light lunches, open sandwiches and delicious home made cakes. A variety of teas, coffees and coffee grinders are on sale. Open all year, seven days a week from 10am to 5pm. Tel: 01492 580908

The Walk

1. Walk along the quay passing the landing stage on the right and the Smallest House in Great Britain on the left. Go through a gap in the town walls and keep ahead to a fork in the lane. Bear right downhill and continue on a wide path along the estuary with boats moored on the right and Bodlondeb Woods behind high walls on the left. Look back for fine views of Conwy Castle. When the path bends to the left there are views across the estuary to Deganwy and, further north, the Great Orme above Llandudno.

2. When the path reaches a road turn left to pass a school. Cross the A547 and keep ahead on a short track to the footbridge that crosses the railway line. On the other side continue on an enclosed track to a lane junction. Turn right and walk uphill along Mountain Road. When the lane forks go right uphill. Just beyond the last house turn right on a narrow path and cross a ladder stile onto Conwy Mountain.

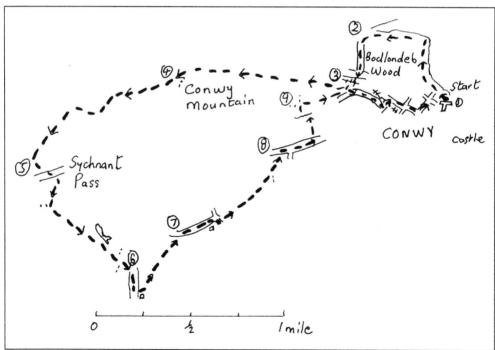

3. Take a clear path uphill through gorse and heather to a col where several paths meet. Follow a path on the right-hand side of the mountain with views to the Great Orme. In places the path follows the ridge, climbing steadily and in about half a mile from the col reaches the remains of an Iron Age hill fort.

The hill fort Castell Caer Seion is approximately 2000 years old. There are about fifty stone huts and house platforms along the ridge and at the west end there is a citadel. When the site was excavated in 1951 the finds included slingstones and querns.

4. Keep ahead on the main path descending in the direction of a farm. About 500 metres from the summit bear right on a narrow path. It soon reaches a post bearing the green North Wales Path Waymark. Go ahead and at the next fork turn left still following the green waymarks. At the next fork bear right and when the path forks again keep ahead to a ford across a stream. There are stepping stones on the left. Continue ahead on a green path. It becomes stony and joins a wider track. Follow it to the head of the Sychnant Pass.

5. Cross the road and go through the gate ahead. With a wall on the left follow the path to a fork. Bear left – the North Wales Path goes

Ponies on Conwy Mountain

to the right here. Continue on a clear path, with the wall still on the left, to a ladder stile. The path passes a pool and reaches a stony track. Bear right and at a fork turn left. Pass the gate to a house on the right and descend a steep track to a lane.

6. Turn right and in about 100 metres turn left through a kissing-gate. Follow the enclosed path through more gates to a field. Cross the field diagonally left to a small gate below trees. Keep ahead to another small gate and leave the next field by a stile. Continue ahead to a corner fence beside a line of trees. Follow the fence on your left. There is a wooded hill on the right. At the end of the field veer closer to the woods and find a kissing-gate amongst the trees.

7. Turn right on the lane and in 300 metres bear left to pass Oakwood Park Hall on the right. Ignore a turning left and curve right to a lane junction. Turn right and in 30 metres go left at a kissing-gate into a field. Follow a hedge nearby on the right through fields. When the hedge bears away to the right keep ahead to a kissing-gate. Turn left to another kissing-gate in the left corner of the field.

8. Turn right along the road and in 450 metres look for a footpath signpost on the left, near a seat. Go through the kissing-gate and walk downhill beside a right-hand fence in the direction of Conwy Mountain. In 200 metres veer left and descend to the left corner of the field. Go through a kissing-gate and cross a footbridge over a stream. An enclosed path leads uphill to a track.

9. Turn right and descend the track through trees. Pass the ladder stile crossed earlier onto Conwy Mountain. Keep ahead and ignore the left track coming from the railway bridge. Bear right following Mountain Road to a T junction. Turn left and follow the road as it bears right and left to cross the railway line. Turn right on the A547 and at the town walls walk through the arch. There are steps on the left here going up onto the walls. Continue along Bangor Road to Lancaster Square and turn left into High Street. Pass Plas Mawr on the left, an Elizabethan house open to the public. Continue to a crossroads. Aberconwy House, a 14th century house owned by the National Trust, is on the right corner. The Lower Arch leading to the quay is straight ahead but to visit Anna's Tea Room or the castle, turn right along Castle Street.

2. Penmaenmawr

Route: An ascending very pleasant path leads to high moorland and the Druid's Circle, a Bronze Age site. On the descent an extension can be taken around Foel Lus following the Jubilee Path, which has magnificent panoramic views.

Distance: 4 or 5½ miles.

How to get there: Penmaenmawr is off the A55, west of Conwy.

Public Transport: Buses from Bangor, Conwy and Llandudno.

Start: Car park in Fernbrook Road, Penmaenmawr.

Maps: Outdoor Leisure 17.

Penmaenmawr is a small seaside resort lying between the huge headlands of Penmaenbach and Penmaenmawr. Before the coming of the railway and modern roads the area was extremely difficult to reach, and leave. Travellers to Anglesey and Bangor who had crossed the Sychnant Pass or risked the tides below Penmaenbach hired local guides to continue around Penmaenmawr. The narrow track, 300 foot above the sea, was liable to landslips and it was usual for coaches to be dismantled and carried to the other side of the headland. Iron Age man occupied the hill for many centuries and Roman coins have been found also the remains of over 100 dwellings. Sadly, quarrying has destroyed the summit, its rock used for making roads and concrete. Penmaenmawr became well known in the 19th century when the town became a favourite resort of William Gladstone.

The Tea Shop

The Oasis Tea Room is also a Christian Bookshop. Hot and cold snacks are served including soup, beans or cheese on toast, tea cakes and scones. Open Monday, Tuesday, Thursday and Friday from 9.30am to 4.30pm. (In the winter, closes at 2pm). Wednesday open 9.30 am to 12.30 p.m. Closed Saturdays and Sundays. Tel: 01492 622322.

The Walk

1. From the car park turn right along Fernbrook Road. Ignore the first road on the right but in a few more paces bear right up a flight of steps. At the top turn right to reach a junction of roads. Bear left and in approximately 20 paces continue ahead on a rough track between fields. In 300 metres the track emerges on Graiglwyd Road near a bridge and stream.

2. Turn right and in 150 metres turn left on a farm access track to Graiglwyd Farm (now kennels). Cross a ladder stile at a gate and in another 50 metres leave the track to keep left, keeping buildings on the right. At the end of the buildings ignore a gate on the left and go uphill to a kissing-gate and a Druid's Circle signpost. After passing a building on the left turn left on a clear path between gorse and trees.

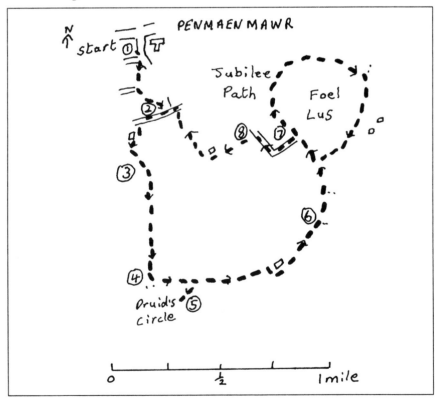

As you ascend there are fine views seawards of the Great Orme and Puffin Island. The hill you are climbing is Graiglwyd, an extinct volcano, on which there was a stone axe factory in Neolithic times. The axes, after polishing, were exported all over Britain. They were probably set in a wooden handle and used to cut down trees. More recent quarrying has destroyed most of the higher slopes of the hill.

3. The path climbs for a while above a wooded valley and in approximately 800 metres a wall is seen ahead on the left. At a path junction continue uphill, parallel with the wall and, after passing a bench, reach another path.

4. At this point, turn left across an old narrow stone bridge and follow the path to a kissing-gate in a wall. Turn right to reach a broad track. Turn left along the track and in about 220 metres look for a path on the right, which leads to the stone circle. The standing stones are clearly visible on the skyline

Although the most famous, the Druid's Circle is only one of many Bronze Age sites on these moorlands. In Welsh the stones are known as Maeni Hirion, meaning long stones. It is thought the circle was used for rituals in the early Bronze Age and excavations revealed three pits in the centre containing cremated bones of children. About 100 metres to the west there is a ring cairn, a low stone circular bank. Excavations suggested that fires had been lit here.

5. Return to the main track and continue eastwards with the sea on

The Druid's Circle

your left. Eventually the track descends to a wall and continues beside it. In 300 metres bear right through a gate in the wall and keep ahead towards pines. At a post with a waymark bear left and pass a house called Bryn Derwydd. Keep ahead through a gate and continue on a clear track following a right-hand wall.

6. In about 360 metres ignore a footpath sign on the right, At this point you also leave the North Wales Path, its green circular discs have waymarked the track across the moorland. This is a long distance route from Prestatyn to Bangor. Do not turn right but keep ahead through a gate and continue to a track junction. Turn left and ignore another track on the right. Descend to a sharp bend at some pillars. Here, if you have the time and energy, you may like to follow the Jubilee Path around Foel Lus.

The Jubilee Path was opened in 1888 commemorating the 1887 Jubilee of Queen Victoria. A fairly level path, it gives superb views of Penmaenmawr, Anglesey, Puffin Island, the Great Orme and the Sychnant Pass. Directly to the north, between Foel Lus and the nearest road, lies Trwyn yr Wylfa, hill of weeping. According to local legend, the prince Helyg and his family escaped to this hill when the sea flooded his palace and land in the bay.

7. To follow the Jubilee Path walk ahead between the pillars onto a wide level path. In about 350 metres the path narrows and there are fine views to the Sychnant Pass. In another 600 metres reach a junction of paths at telephone poles. Turn right uphill to follow the lines. The path levels out and reaches an access track coming from a farm. Keeping a wall on the left continue on the track. When the wall bends left, keep uphill and pass a grassy track on the left. In another 40 metres bear right on a grassy path through heather. Ignore another path climbing the hill on the right and descend gradually to the track walked earlier. Turn right to the start of the Jubilee Path. Bear left at the bend and descend Mountain Lane, passing a cattle grid. Continue past houses on the right and, in another 150 metres, turn left up steps to a kissing-gate.

8. Follow a fence on the right and pass above a farm. Keep ahead to join a track above a reservoir. Cross a stile on the right and bear left following a fence as it bends right. Ignore a kissing-gate on the left. In another 50 metres go through a kissing-gate onto a surfaced track. Continue ahead to a lane and turn left. In a few paces turn right on the track between fields walked earlier to retrace your steps to the start in Penmaenmawr.

3. Llanfairfechan

Route: This lovely walk, which climbs steadily up the lower slopes of the Carneddau Mountains to almost 400 metres, offers magnificent views of the North Wales coast and Anglesey. Although mostly on good tracks and paths, some care is needed in following the correct route off the moorland.

Distance: 5½ miles.

How to get there: Llanfairfechan is off the A55 between Conwy and Bangor.

Public Transport: Frequent buses from Bangor, Conwy and Llandudno. Some trains on the Chester-Holyhead line stop at Llanfairfechan.

Start: Car park in Station Road, Llanfairfechan.

Maps: Outdoor Leisure 17.

Tea Shop

Bont y Castell is near the traffic lights in Aber Road. A warm welcome is extended to walkers and the varied menu includes all day breakfast, jacket potatoes, toasties and scones with jam or cream. Open all year, except Sundays, from 10.00am to 4.00pm.

The North Wales Path above Llanfairfechan

The Walk

1. From the car park turn left along Station Road. Cross Aber Road
at the traffic lights and keep ahead up Village Road. Ignore a footpath signpost between the Midland Bank and the school.. Follow
the road past the school and bear right over a bridge to cross afon
Llanfairfechan.

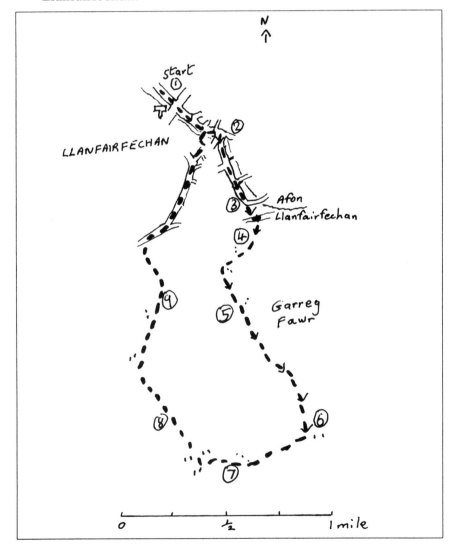

2. Immediately turn left to pass the Llanfair Arms on you right and, in about 300 metres, pass a bridge on the left. Continue along Nant y Felin Road and, in 100 metres, ignore a footpath signpost on the right. Follow the road another 300 metres and look for a house called Blaen Nant on the right. After passing the house, and before the lane bends left to cross a bridge, turn right towards some steps.

3. Go up the steps and reach a lane. Turn left to have superb views towards the coast. In 100 metres turn right through a kissing-gate and cross the field diagonally right to a ladder stile and an enclosed track. The track bears left and goes directly uphill to another stile.

4. Take a clear path to the right slanting uphill. Keep a look-out for scrubland and moorland birds such as stonechats and wheatears. Looking towards the coast, there are fine views of Anglesey and Puffin Island. Stay on the main path, passing a seat in about 250 metres. Go through a kissing-gate and keep ahead. On the right, off the path, there are remains of hut circles. Keep ahead and cross another track. On this section of the walk the route follows the North Wales Path, a long distance path from Prestatyn to Bangor, and you may see some of its green waymarks.

5. With the hill known as Garreg Fawr on the left reach a wall on the right, which is followed until it descends. After another 10 metres, where the track forks, go left uphill. Ignore a lesser path on the left. When a wall is visible on your left, keep ahead towards a stony track. On reaching the track, go ahead and, just before some pylons, bear left at a fork. Continue to a track junction.

The track on your left passes through Bwlch Ddeulfaen, the line of the Roman road from Segontium, near Caernarfon to Canovium, at Caerhun in the Conwy valley.

6. At the track junction turn right and pass another track on the right. Keep ahead downhill and after following this stony track for 550 metres look for a green path on the left, which continues in the same direction as before but above the track.

On this area of moorland you may see semi-domesticated ponies which are allowed to run wild and graze on the slopes of the Carneddau mountains.

7. Follow the path for 400 metres and then bear right downhill on another path. Cross the lower track and head towards a coniferous plantation. Go under the wires of pylons and pass a walled enclosure on your right. Follow a path to a gate near a junction of walls.

8. Go through the gate and follow a wall on the left. Cross a stream, go through another gate and take a rough track downhill with a wall on the left and coniferous woodland on the right. Pass a ruined house on the left and in another 160 metes, where the track forks, bear right uphill. In 100 metres, at a corrugated building, bear right to a kissing-gate. Keep ahead slightly to the left and go through a gap in a wall. Descend the field diagonally to a kissing-gate near a broad gate at some trees.

9. Keep ahead on a track and, after passing through another kissing-gate, ignore a track on the left coming from a farm. The track bears right to reach a lane. Turn right and at a fork bear left downhill along Llanerch Road. In 600 metres, near a cemetery, turn right. After passing a road called Pen-y-Bryn on your right, turn left through a kissing-gate. Follow a path between small fields and descend to a bridge across afon Llanfairfechan. Cross and bear left on the road passing the Midland Bank. Go ahead to Aber Road, Bont y Castell and the car park.

4. Trefriw

Route: A superb varied walk with long but gentle climbs. An ascent through woodland leading to an ancient church is followed by more uphill paths with wonderful views. The hillside descent passes the lake Llyn Geirionydd.

Distance: 5½ miles.

How to get there: Trefriw is on the B5106, south of Conwy.

Public Transport: Buses from Llanrwst and Llandudno. Trains to Llanrwst from Llandudno Junction and Blaenau Ffestiniog.

Start: Car parking along the lane opposite the Trefriw Woollen Mill.

Maps: Outdoor Leisure 17.

Trefriw is a large village sited where afon Crafnant flows into the Conwy. For centuries dominated by farming, Trefriw became an important port in the 18th and 19th centuries when lead ore and slate from local mines and quarries were shipped down-river to Conwy for export on larger vessels. By the late 19th century thousands of people were coming upriver in paddle steamers to visit the iron rich springs north of the village. Trefriw flourished as a spa until the start of the First World War. Paddle steamer trips continued for about another 20 years until silt stopped them travelling so far up the river. The woollen mill was originally a fulling mill used by local people to wash their cloth. At first the mill was powered by water wheels. Hydro electricity has now taken over.

The Tea Shops

There are two possibilities. For the first, after looking around the Trefriw Woollen Mill you may like to have refreshments in the tea room next to the shop. It is possible to make a tour of the mill seeing the many processes involved in weaving. In the summer there is a hand-spinning demonstration. Do not miss the weavers' garden. The tea room is self service with a choice of sandwiches and cakes. Open all year (except for Christmas and New Year holidays) weekdays 9.30am to 5pm (4.30pm in winter). Saturdays 10am to 4.30pm (4pm Winter). Sundays open Easter and May holidays, late May to end of September 2pm to 4. 30pm. Tel: 01492 640462.

Glanrafon Stores Tea Room. This is a general store with a small tea room and pavement tables. The menu includes hot snacks, all day breakfast, Welsh cream teas and home-made tray bakes. Open all year from early morning to 7pm (4pm on Sundays). Tel: 01492 642 177.

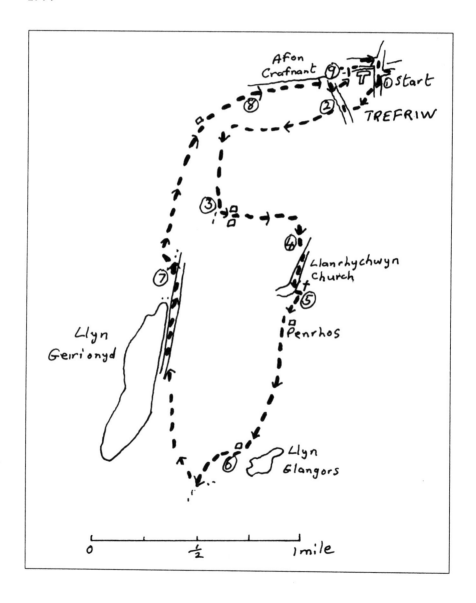

The Walk

1. From the car park walk out to the B5106 and turn left. Take the first lane on the right and in 200 metres bear left at a fork. When the lane turns left keep ahead on a path between a fence and hedge. On reaching a lane turn right and pass a house. Turn left at a footpath signpost.

2. Follow the path as it rises through woodland. The path climbs onto a rocky hill with fine views and then continues into more trees. At a fork near a wall turn left to have the wall on your right.

3. Follow the wall past a corner and continue beside a fence. Go through a gap and walk uphill with a fence on the right to a stile. Walk behind buildings and go through a gate. Keep ahead on a track and bear left to go through another gate. At a footpath signpost ignore the right fork and continue ahead on the track through rough pasture and marsh. The track becomes surfaced and reaches a lane.

4. Turn right and where the lane bends right to Llyn Geirionydd, keep ahead on a track. In 100 metres, where the track bends right, bear slightly left in the direction of Tyn Llan. Almost immediately turn left to reach a kissing-gate and walk through the field to Llanrhychwyn Church.

Llanrhychwyn Church

Llanrhychwyn Church may be the oldest church in Wales. In the 6th century a Celtic saint, Saint Rhychwyn, founded a church here but nothing remains of the original wooden building. The doorway and surrounding walls are the oldest parts of the present church, 11th or 12th century. Maredudd ap Ieuan of Dolwyddelan may have built the north aisle in the 16th century. The font is very old and there is some medieval glass. Llywelyn the Great had a court in the Conwy Valley and he worshipped here with his wife Princess Joan, daughter of King John. Because his wife found the walk to this church tiring, Llywelyn had a church built in Trefriw.

5. Return through the kissing-gate to the track and bear left. Go through a gate and pass Penrhos on the left. Keep ahead to reach a ladder stile. The original track becomes blocked and the path veers away from the wall through gorse and small trees. After passing through a gap in a wall, bear right to reach another ladder stile. Go ahead and follow the path through a valley to reach a stile near a gate. Bear slightly right to pass a ruin on the right. At the end of a wall descend slightly left on a visible path. You will see a plantation and a lake – Llyn Glangors – below on your left. Go through a gate and follow a track. Cross a stile to the left of a gate and pass in front of a house called Castell y Gwynt.

6. Cross another stile and keep ahead on the track. Go through a gate to pass the disused New Pandora lead and zinc mine. In a few metres bear right passing mine tips to have a fence on your right. Cross a ladder stile and descend a clear path through heather with superb views of Llyn Geirionydd below. This lake is polluted with lead and has no fish. On reaching the lane beside the lake turn right through a gate and keep ahead beside the lake. At the end of the lake ignore a kissing-gate and continue to a ladder stile on the left.

7. Follow the path and cross another ladder stile. At a fork go left descending on a clear path. It bends to the left and join.. another path. Go right to reach a stile. On the opposite bank of the nearby stream stands the gaunt ruins of the New Pandora Mine processing works. Join a track and keep ahead through woodland. Continue past the hedged Plas Eengan to reach a gate and bridge at afon Crafnant.

8. Do not go through the gate ahead to cross the bridge. Take a path on the right between walls and go through a small gate in a hedge

on the right. Keep ahead above the river to pass through a gap into the next field. Keep ahead through trees then follow a fence. Leave the fields via a kissing-gate and bear left to follow a road to a junction near a bridge.

9. Turn right on the road and take the first lane left. In 30 metres go left in front of a terrace of houses and follow a path between walls. At a path junction turn left to cross a bridge over afon Crafnant and immediately turn left through a kissing-gate. Descend to the river and at a waterfall bear left to have the river on your right. Go through a kissing-gate and ignore a footbridge on the right. Bear left between walls to a lane. Bear right to the B5106. Turn right passing Glanrafon Stores Tea Room and keep ahead to Trefriw Mill and the start of the walk.

5. Llyn Crafnant

Route: A superb walk beside two lovely lakes. There is some climbing and short sections of the path are quite rocky.

Distance: 5 miles.

How to get there: From Conwy take the B5106 to Trefriw. Opposite the Fairy Falls Hotel take a lane signposted Llyn Crafnant. Large car park on the right in just over 2 miles.

Public Transport: Nearest bus stop in Trefriw.

Start: Forestry car park near Llyn Crafnant.

Maps: Outdoor Leisure 17.

The Tea Shop

The Lakeside Café at Cynllwyd Mawr beside Llyn Crafnant has a small tea room and sheltered tea garden in a beautiful setting beside the lake. A varied menu includes lunches, soup, baked potatoes and home-made cakes. Open from the end of March to the end of October, every day 8a.m to 6pm.

The tea garden beside Llyn Crafnant

The Walk

1. Leave the car park by walking out through the entrance. Cross the lane to a forest track and bear left to follow the track uphill through coniferous trees. At a wide area, where the track bears right, keep ahead to a stile. Follow the path to the workings of a quarry.

Clogwyn Fuwch slate quarry is a small, mainly underground quarry with workings on six levels. It may have started operating as early as the 18th century but output was never large and most of the slate was used locally.

2. Stay on the main path and pass mine buildings on your right. When the path reaches a fork take the path downhill over rough ground. Go through a gap in a broken wall and follow the path through birch trees. It rises gently to a ladder stile. Cross the stile and continue on a clear path uphill to pass coniferous trees on your right. Go through a gap in a wall and climb the hill on your left to reach the monument to Taliesin.

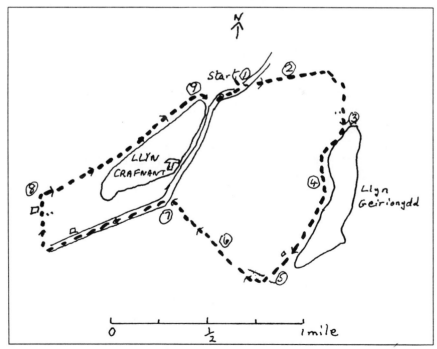

Taliesin was a bard who lived in the 6th century near Llyn Geirionydd. The monument was placed here in 1850. Thirteen years later this spot became the location for an Eisteddfod which was held annually and organised by the rebel bard Gwilym Cowlyd. He won the Chair in 1861 at the Eisteddfod when it was held in Conwy, but disagreement over the rules led to his running of a rival Eisteddfod until his death in 1904. His associates continued with the event until 1912.

3. Descend the hill in the direction of the lake, Llyn Geirionydd.
    Bear left to go through a gap in a wall near a barn. Turn right and
    pass the barn on your left. Follow a wall on your right to a ladder
    stile. With the lake on your left continue on a rough path. The
    water in the lake is polluted with lead from nearby rocks and it
    contains no fish. Water skiers and canoeists practise their sports
    here. Pass a fenced area at a lead and zinc mine adit and follow
    the path above the lake.

4. Before the end of the headland bear right uphill and scramble
    down some rocks to the shore again. With the lake nearby on
    your left follow the path through the trees. Many of the conifers
    are larches. At the end of the woods, cross a stile and keep ahead
    through a field. The path veers away from the lake and goes
    through a gap in a wall to pass below a house. Cross a stile to
    reach a track.

5. Turn right and follow the track uphill. After the track crosses a
    stream, and before the track bends right, bear right on a steep
    path uphill. Rejoin the track and cross to another path. When the
    path reaches the track again, keep ahead uphill on a wide path.
    At the next track turn right about 10 metres to a track junction.
    Bear left and in 50 metres, where the track bends right, keep
    ahead on a narrow path.

6. Go through a gap in a wall and follow a fairly level path through
    dense coniferous trees. In 50 metres the path begins its descent
    to a stile and continues downhill, soon with a stream on the left.
    Ignore a stile ahead and bear left to cross the stream. Follow the
    path to a ladder stile and lane. The walk continues to the left but,
    if you want to visit the café now, turn right for 300 metres. It is on
    the left.

7. Turn left on the lane. (If you visit the café, return to this point to

finish the walk). Follow the lane through a gate. Pass a house and go through another gate. Ignore the track uphill and turn right. Cross a bridge and in another 20 metres bear right to cross a footbridge. Do not cross the stile ahead but turn left through a gate. Follow the path uphill through trees to a ladder stile near a waterfall.

8. Turn right and take the rough track downhill. Continue through the forest and keep ahead with the lake, Llyn Geirionydd, on your right.

This lake is not polluted. It contains fish and you may see mallards, mergansers and wagtails. Because the lake is a reservoir, bathing is not allowed but boats may be hired at the café.

9. At the end of the lake turn right through a gate to the lane. The monument nearby commemorates the giving of the lake as a water supply to the community of Llanrwst. Turn left to return to the car park, or right to visit the tea garden.

6. Llanrwst

Route: A varied walk starting with a riverside stroll and continuing with a gradual climb on quiet paths through the lovely Gwydr forest. There are several interesting features along the way.

Distance: 5½ miles.

How to get there: Llanrwst is on the A470, south of Llandudno, north of Betws y Coed. At the town, cross the old bridge to reach the car park on the B5106.

Public Transport: Trains from Llandudno Junction and Blaenau Ffestiniog.

Start: Car park near the recreation ground on the B5106, west side of the River Conwy.

Maps: Outdoor Leisure 17.

The Tea Shop

Covered with Virginia creeper, Tu Hwnt I'r Bont is a lovely old building dating back to the 15th century when it was used as a court-room. It is now owned by the National Trust. New and second-hand books are on sale upstairs whilst the tea room is on the ground floor.

The tea room near the River Conwy

The food is home-made and light lunches and cream teas are served. Welsh Rarebit is made to a special recipe and there is a delicious selection of cakes. Open Tuesday before Easter until the end of October from 10am to 5.30pm. Closed Mondays except Bank Holidays.

The Walk

Llanrwst is a small market town in the Conwy valley. Designed by the famous architect Inigo Jones, Pont Fawr, the beautiful bridge spanning the river, was built in 1636. A chapel attached to the parish church is of interest. It contains the ornate coffin of Llywelyn the Great and a 15th century effigy of Hywel Coetmor, one of Llywelyn's descendants.

1. From the car park walk past the children's playground and keep ahead towards the River Conwy. Turn right on the riverside path and go through a kissing-gate. As you walk along you may hear the sound of peacocks from the gardens of Gwydyr Castle, which is across the fields on your right.

The building was originally a fortified Tudor mansion and home of the locally important Wynn family. Following fire damage in the 1920s the property has been restored. It is open to the public.

2. In about 700 metres cross a stile into a field and turn right to follow a fence. Go through the field gate onto the road. Turn right and in 100 metres turn left on a forestry road signposted Gwydyr Uchaf Chapel. Follow the road as it bends right and ignore a forestry track on the left. Pass a small parking area and turn left to pass the chapel on your left.

Gwydyr Uchaf Chapel was a private chapel built in the 17th century for Sir Richard Wynn when the family had two homes in Llanrwst, one at Gwydyr and another near the chapel. The exterior is quite plain but the decoration inside is amazing. Extraordinary paintings cover the entire ceiling. It is possible to go in the chapel during weekday office hours when the nearby Forestry offices are open.

3. From the chapel door follow a wide path to a stile and field. Keep ahead to another stile and reach a wide forest track. Turn right to have fine views over the Conwy Valley. In about 400 metres look for yellow topped posts on the left and follow a steep path uphill

through mixed woods. When you reach another path bear right for 150 metres to a track. Keep straight ahead in the direction of a yellow-topped post and follow a path through the forest until you reach a broad track.

4. Turn right downhill to a track junction. Cross to the opposite track and follow it for 800 metres until, after bending right, it reaches a lane near the Hafna mine. Turn left uphill and, in approximately 80 metres, turn right to pass a barrier onto a track. Almost immediately turn left on a path. Before taking the path look for an information board on your right.

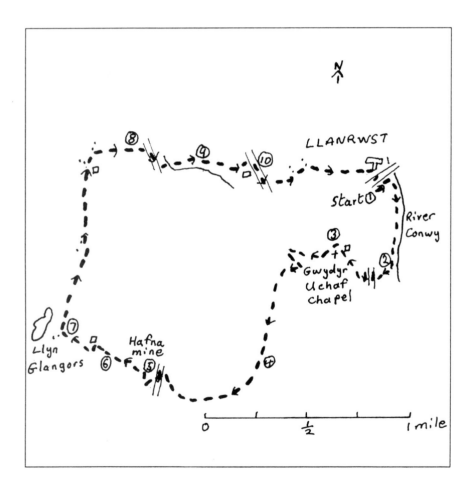

Lead mining has operated in the Gwydr forest for nearly 400 years. The Hafna lead and zinc mine mill operated from 1879 until about 1915. With the help of the interpretative panels it is possible to locate the smelting house, slime pit, crushing floor, line of chimney flue etc. It is probably the most interesting site in the area. Deep mine shafts accessible from the paths and tracks have been capped to ensure safety for walkers and other wanderers. They have grills at the side to allow bats the use of mine workings for roosting, hibernation and breeding. You may have noticed hammer and pick discs along part of the route. These are waymarks for a two-mile Miner's Trail, which starts near Llyn Sarnau.

5. The path ascends to mine building ruins. Look on your right for another information panel. Continue on the path, which is stepped in places. Pass a tall chimney on the left and reach a stile. Bear right on the track until it bends right. Here, leave the track to keep ahead, slightly to the right, on a narrow path. It goes uphill between gorse and trees. Climb a ladder stile and continue on another path. Cross a track and continue uphill following a line of telephone wires. Pass a stile and cottage and keep ahead with conifers on the left and a field on the right. Ignore another stile on the right and cross the stile ahead.

6. Continue with a wall on the left to a stile opposite a house. Turn left on a track and in about 30 metres turn right over a rough stile. Follow a wall on the right and in a few paces look for a narrow path on the left. Follow it through heather to a stile. Continue beside a wall and descend to a track. The route turns right here but if you wish to see Llyn Glangors follow the path opposite for about 150 metres to the lakeside.

This attractive lake is an artificial reservoir constructed to provide a water supply for a nearby lead mine. Nowadays it is stocked with trout.

7. Return to the track and turn left and follow it to a fork. Turn left and in approximately 500 metres, shortly before the track bears right, look for a yellow arrow on a tree on the left. Take a narrow path through the forest and in 50 metres ignore a stile on the left. The path reaches an old quarrying area and descends between fences to a track. Turn left and 50 metres beyond a house bear right to go through a field gate. Follow the left boundary of the field to the next gate. Continue on a track through trees and on

reaching an open field keep ahead to another gate. A green track through deciduous trees leads to a field. Follow the right boundary closely to reach a broken wall on the left and continue on an enclosed track to a stile. Keep ahead beside the left wall to a lane.

8. Turn right on the lane for about 150 metres. At a footpath signpost on the left, descend a steep path, following it to a stream. Cross the footbridge and follow the waymarked trees on a clear path downhill through the woods and emerge on a track. Turn left and in a few paces you will see on the right a stile with a yellow arrow. Trees have been felled at the bottom of the woods and because of this you may reach the track at a different point. The stile is about 20 metres from where the stream crosses the track.

9. Go through the gate and follow a clear path to a kissing-gate. Keep ahead with the stream at first nearby on the right. Bear left to follow a wall on your left. Keep it a few metres distant. Descend the path and in the bottom left-hand corner of this rough field you will find a low broken stile. Cross and bear right to a better stile. Follow an enclosed path to the B5106.

10. Turn right and in 150 metres turn left over a stile at a footpath signpost. Cross an embankment and follow the left-hand fence through the field to a stile and track. Keep ahead. Ignore a stile on the left. The track bends right and eventually joins the B5106 near the bridge and tea room.

7. Llanberis

Route: A fairly easy walk with many interesting features. These include Llyn Padarn, Dolbadarn Castle, a stretch of moorland and Ceunant Mawr waterfalls.

Distance: 3½ miles.

How to get there: Llanberis is on the A4086 between Caernarfon and Capel Curig.

Public Transport: Buses from Caernarfon and Bangor. Snowdon Sherpa service from Betws y Coed.

Start: Car park near Llyn Padarn on the A4086.

Maps: Outdoor Leisure 17.

The Tea Shop

Cegin Eryri Tea Room has its own traditional bakery next door. Hot snacks are available and Welsh afternoon teas. Specialities include Welsh cakes and bara brith. Packed lunches can be provided if ordered – by phone – in advance. Open all year Monday to Saturday 9am to 4.30pm. Easter and summer holidays open on Sundays 11am to 4pm. Tel: 01286 870491.

The Walk

1. From the car park walk towards Llyn Padarn and turn right to have the lake on your left. Cross a footbridge and keep ahead over grass.

Llyn Padarn is a very attractive lake and being two miles long it is one of the largest in Snowdonia. The arctic char, the torgoch, lives in its deepest waters. Slate quarrying took place on a big scale here on the southern flanks of Mynydd Elidir, leaving behind inclines, terraces and pits. Surrounded by sessile oak woodland, a former quarry hospital stands above the northern shore. Situated in the Llyn Padarn Country Park it is open to visitors. Other attractions are short walking trails, a museum and a lakeside narrow gauge railway.

2. Go through a kissing-gate in a fence and maintain your direction to cross a track above a ditch. Head towards Dolbadarn Castle on its rocky hill. After crossing a gravel path go ahead and follow a

fence on the right to a kissing-gate and enter a car park. Leave by
the main entrance and cross the road. Descend steps to a footbridge over afon Arddu. Go up steps and follow a rough path to a
wall gap at a hut. To look around the castle ruins go through the
kissing-gate ahead. (At the time of writing there is no charge).

Dolbadarn Castle stands on a rocky knoll between Llyn Padarn and Llyn
Peris. It was probably built by Llywelyn ap Iorwerth (the Great) in the early
years of the 13th century. There were other buildings on the site and materi-
als from these may have been re-used in Edward I's castle at Caernarfon. In
the 15th century, during the uprising of Owain Glyndwr, the castle was used
to imprison Owain's enemy Lord Grey of Ruthin.
The castle stands above Llyn Peris. It is probable that thousands of years
ago there was only one lake and debris carried by afon Arddu formed a delta

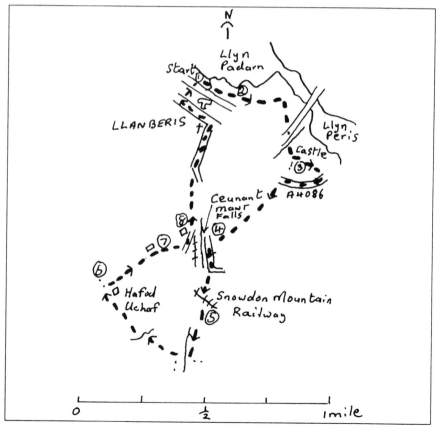

separating the lakes Padarn and Peris. In the 18th century, the lakes were used to transport copper from the Nant Peris mine. The chief carrier of the ore was an elderly woman called Margaret Ferch Evan who built her own boats. She was also a musician and a wrestler. Llyn Peris is used as the lower reservoir for the water of the Dinorwig Power Station. Water from lake Llyn Marchlyn Mawr, situated at nearly 2000 feet, flows through tunnels in the mountain Elidir Fawr generating electricity. The water continues to Llyn Padarn and is stored until low peak times when it is pumped back up to the higher lake.

3. Leaving the castle go through the kissing-gate but before reaching the wall turn left. Follow a rough path downhill through a kissing-gate and keep ahead to the A4086. Turn right and pass a chapel and cottages on your right. Cross a ladder stile at a footpath signpost on the left. Follow the track as it winds uphill through the forest. It becomes steeper then narrows to pass below a house. Cross a stile and emerge on a lane.

4. Turn left uphill to pass a cottage. Where the lane bends left turn right through a gap in the wall. Follow a wall on your left. Continue on a clear path and keep ahead to a stile beside the line of the Snowdon Mountain Railway.

The Snowdon Mountain Railway climbs for nearly five miles from Llanberis to the top of Snowdon, ascending over 3000 feet on the way. The only rack and pinion railway in Britain it is narrow gauge (2ft 7in) with a maximum gradient of 1 in 5. On the day of opening in 1896 there was a fatal accident when the carriage separated from the locomotive which had been pulling it. The carriage ran downhill and came to a halt with no fatalities but one man had panicked and jumped to his death.

5. After crossing the line follow a clear path through moorland. Look for cotton grass in spring and listen for the poignant sound of the curlew. Snowdon is ahead to your left. The path goes through a gap in a wall and in about 50 metres bears right to cross a bridge over afon Arddu. After crossing the river keep ahead on a track. Ignore a lesser path on your left. Reach a ladder stile at a gate and turn right on a track. Cross a bridge over afon Hwch. Continue on the track as it bears left between walls. Ignore a stile on the right. Pass a house in trees and immediately bear right over a stile next to a gate at the head of a lane.

6. Continue beside a fence on the right and shortly bear right on a track towards a house called Hafod Uchaf. In a few paces turn left to follow a wall on your right. Go through a kissing-gate in a crossing wall and keep ahead following the remains of a wall on your left. Cross a stream and go ahead to the next kissing-gate. Continue beside a broken wall and stream to cross a plank bridge at a red topped post. Bear right to a track and turn left descending to a kissing-gate next to a broad gate.

7. Turn right on an access track and descend to a lane. On the right a kissing-gate across the narrow gauge line gives access to afon Arddu above waterfalls. Descend the lane and just before a house go through a kissing-gate on the right to a viewpoint of Ceunant Mawr waterfalls.

8. Pass the house and shortly turn left on a footpath through trees. When the path joins a track turn left and pass a wall on the right. In another 20 metres take a path on the right. Cross a stream and go through a kissing-gate. Follow a fence on the left and pass a house. Continue through more kissing-gates and descend steps to a lane. Turn left and pass a church on the left. When you reach a road turn left. The Cegin Eryri Tea Room is on your right. To return to the car park continue along the road beyond the tea room and in another 100 metres turn right at a footpath signpost. At the A4086 turn right to the car park.

Ceunant Mawr waterfalls

8. Capel Curig

Route: A fairly easy walk with magnificent lake and mountain views. There is some rough ground and short stretches of track and path may be wet or muddy.

Distance: 4 miles.

How to get there: Capel Curig is on the A5 between Betws y Coed and Bethesda.

Public Transport: Buses from Caernarfon, Llandudno and Betws y Coed.

Start: Car park behind the General Stores in Capel Curig.

Maps: Outdoor Leisure 17

Situated in the heart of north Snowdonia, Capel Curig is popular with walkers and tourists who enjoy mountain landscapes. Moel Siabod dominates the scene to the south and from hill slopes above the village there are magnificent views of the Snowdon range.

Llynau Mymbyr, near Capel Curig

The Tea Shop

The Pinnacle Café is in the same building as an outdoor shop and the village post office and general stores. The varied menu includes hot snacks and afternoon teas including home-made Welsh cakes. Open all year. Winter hours 8.30am to 4.30pm. Closes at 6pm or later in the summer. Tel: 01690 720201.

The Walk

1. From the car park turn right and follow a track. This is an old road built in the 15th century by the owner of a Bethesda slate quarry and it is a right of way almost to Llyn Ogwen. In 250 metres pass a house on the left and keep ahead through a gate. In another 100 metres bear left on a track which passes above a ruined barn.

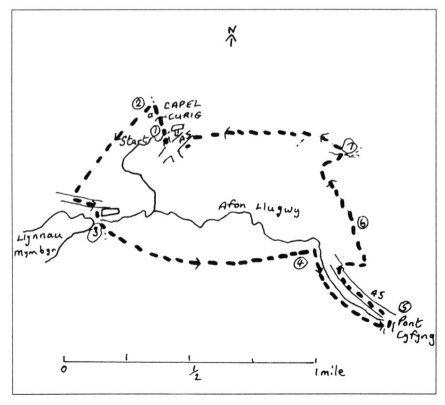

2. At a fork take the left track and pass directly behind the house. Continue on a broad track and in 700 metres cross a track and keep ahead to a ladder stile on the A4086. Cross the road and turn left. In 100 metres, turn right over a ladder stile.

Looking west there is a splendid view of Snowdon with Llynnau Mymbyr in the foreground. A delta has developed halfway along the lake almost splitting it in two. On your left are the grounds of Plas y Brenin. Originally called the Capel Curig Inn, the building was built about 1800 by Pennant, the slate quarry owner from Bethesda. The inn became popular with tourists and after a visit from Queen Victoria the name was changed to the Royal Hotel. The hotel closed in 1953 and reopened two years later as the Plas y Brenin Mountain Centre.

3. Follow a path over a footbridge to reach a wide track. Turn left through mixed woods. Pass houses on the left and in another 600 metres at a fork take the right-hand track. The track becomes rough and reaches afon Llugwy. Follow a fence on the left up steps and above a gorge. Stay on the main path until you reach a footpath signpost, which is about 30 metres before a footbridge.

4. At the signpost bear right down the hill towards the river. On reaching the bottom of the slope, bear right and soon follow the river on your left. Cross a ladder stile into a field and continue beside the river. Go through a gap in a wall and keep ahead. Pass a barn and before the end of the field bear right to cross a footbridge. At a wall turn left to emerge on a track. Bear left and when the track reaches a lane turn left over a bridge called Pont Cyfyng.

In the early 19ᵗʰ century, before the building of the A5, the lane and bridge carried mail coaches on their journey between London and Holyhead.

5. Turn left and follow the A5 past the Tyn y Coed Hotel. Just before reaching a school turn right over a ladder stile. Follow the path as it winds uphill through woodland to a path junction. Turn left and pass above a school. Continue uphill to a ladder stile.

6. Keep ahead and cross the field in the direction of an isolated tree. Cross a grassy track and go through a gap beside the tree. Continue to a ladder stile and reach a fence. Follow the fence to a track and continue to a gate on the right. Keep ahead on a grassy track. In 20 metres bear right to follow a fence. Cross a ladder

stile and go ahead to reach open ground. Cross a small stream and in another 50 metres cross a stone slab bridge.

7. Turn left and go through a gap in the wall to have superb views of Moel Siabod and Snowdon. Cross a ladder stile and ignore a path on the left. Continue on a stony path below a rocky hill called Clogwyn Mawr. The path passes through birch and oak trees to reach a stile. Continue on a clear path over boggy ground. Keep to the right of a rocky wooded knoll and descend to a track. Turn left over a stream and go through a gap in a wood. Descend to a ladder stile on the A5 near the Pinnacle Café and lane to the start.

9. Betws y Coed

Route: This fairly strenuous walk starts with a steep climb through the Gwydr Forest to a lonely lake on a high plateau. The route then follows gentler paths through forest and pasture before returning to the valley and following afon Llugwy.

Distance: 6½ miles.

How to get there: Betws y Coed is on the A5 near the junction with the A470.

Public Transport: Trains from Llandudno Junction stop at Betws y Coed on their way to Blaenau Ffestiniog.

Start: Betws y Coed Railway Station. Car parks nearby.

Maps: Outdoor Leisure 17.

Situated in a narrow wooded valley near the meeting of the Conwy and Llugwy rivers, Betws y Coed has grown from being a point on the London to Holyhead road to a well known tourist resort. First popular with the Victorians through the painting of the water colour artist David Cox and the arrival of the railway, the village continues to attract many visitors. The crowds are soon left behind, however, on this walk that climbs quickly out of the valley.

The Tea Shops

From the many refreshment places in Betws y Coed I have selected two. **The Alpine Coffee Shop** in the old station buildings has a varied menu including hot dishes and home-made pancakes. It is usually closed for a short period during the winter. Summer hours 9.30am to 5.30pm. Tel: 01690 710747. **The Buffet Coach Café** is a railway coach at the Railway Museum. The menu includes hot snacks and Welsh cream teas. Open 7 days a week Easter to the end of October. 10. 30 am to 5.30 p.m. Open Saturday and Sunday the remainder of the year. Tel: 01690 710568.

The Walk

1. With your back to the railway station entrance turn left and walk towards the A5. Before reaching the main road turn right to follow a path through the village green. Continue on the pavement and in 150 metres bear right to cross Pont y Pair, a 15th century stone bridge crossing afon Llugwy. Immediately turn left.

On the rocks near the river you may be able to find three rock cannons. There is an information panel on a wall that has a Snowdonia Park sign. The smallest cannon, with only seven holes, is near a telephone pole. The largest one is nearer the river. The holes are connected to each other by narrow channels which form a fire channel when they are charged with black powder and the first one ignited. They are fired on very special occasions such as the Investiture of a Prince of Wales.

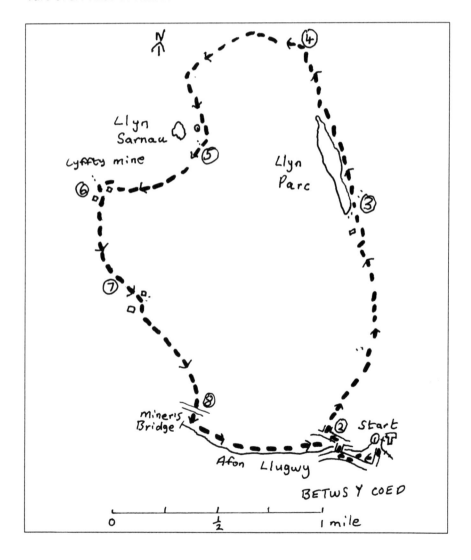

2. Walk uphill and in about 100 metres turn right on a road signed No Through Road. Where the road bends sharp left, take the second track on the right, uphill. When the track levels and starts to descend look for a narrow path on the left. Follow it uphill through conifers. At a junction of paths keep ahead. The path levels for a short distance before climbing alongside a stream tumbling through a rocky ravine. You will pass remains of the Aberllyn lead and zinc mine. It closed in 1921. Follow a path alongside a field and pass the gate to a cottage. Join a track and keep ahead to another track above Llyn Parc.

This is a natural lake but in the early years of the 20th century it was enlarged to drive turbines for the mines. Some of the mine chambers are actually beneath the lake. Because of the presence of lead there are no fish.

3. Cross the track to descend to the lakeside and bear right to walk beside the lake. Follow yellow topped posts along this delightful path which winds in and out of the trees. In late summer bilberries may be found here. At the end of lake the path bears right uphill to meet a track. Turn left and when the track forks bear left to go downhill. In about 200 metres turn left on a wide path.

4. In 50 metres the path reaches an open stony piece of land. Keep ahead and enter deciduous trees to follow a narrow path. The path descends past two fenced off areas bearing left, slightly uphill through mixed woods. The path meets another fence, goes through a broken wall and reaches a track. Turn right and at a track junction turn left. Llyn Sarnau can be seen through the trees on the right.

The lake was constructed during the middle of the 19th century to provide water for a nearby lead mine. Nowadays, Llyn Sarnau is often dry.

5. When the track forks turn right and in 20 metres at a junction keep ahead to take a track directly opposite. As the track descends a cottage can be seen ahead. In about 200 metres turn right over a ladder stile and follow a stone wall. When the wall bears away to the right continue on the clear path following walking man waymarks. There are fine views towards Moel Siabod. When the path reaches a wall continue beside it to a fence near a house. Keep the fence on the left and continue to a track. Cross the track and follow the wall for about 50 metres be-

fore going through a gap. The walk turns left here but you may first like to visit the remains of the Cyffty lead mine. The ruined buildings are about 150 metres to the right. The site has several information plaques.

Miner's Bridge, near Betws y Coed

6. Turning left walk across the field passing a marker post and a building on the left. Continue along a track and cross a ladder stile. Pass a ruined barn and an old farmhouse. Follow a green path directly ahead and downhill. There are wonderful views as the path bears slightly left to descend to a ladder stile at deciduous trees. Follow the left edge of the field towards coniferous forest. When the trees are nearby on the left, the path veers away from the fence to cross a ladder stile. Turn left on a grassy track and cross another stile near a gate. Keep ahead to a wide-open area and turn right on a grassy track that narrows to a footpath through the forest. Foxgloves grow here in summer. Cross a stile at the edge of the forest.

7. Keep ahead across a field and pass a rocky outcrop on the left. Pass to the right of a ruined barn and reach a track. Follow a wall on the right as it bends right and descends a rough path with blue topped posts. Leave the wall where it bends right to pass rocky outcrops with a cottage behind them. Bear left to reach a wall on the right and descend to a ladder stile. Follow a steep path downhill, which can be slippery after rain. In about 50 metres the path becomes wider with more comfortable walking on a bed of pine needles. Cross a footbridge, pass a seat, cross over a grassy ride and reach a lane.

8. Cross directly over the lane and descend a steep path downhill to afon Llugwy and the Miner's Bridge. The first bridge here was built to provide a short cut for the miners living across the river who worked in the lead mines on the plateau. Do not cross the bridge but bear left to follow a fence above the river. When the fence ends continue to a ladder stile and field. Follow the path alongside the river and cross a footbridge. Continue to a ladder stile and pass through more woodland before reaching Pont y Pair. Retrace your steps to the railway station.

10. Conwy Falls and Capel Garmon

Route: This interesting walk starts by following an old toll road above afon Conwy. Ascending woodland paths and quiet lanes lead to a Neolithic burial chamber.

Distance: 4 miles.

How to get there: Two miles south of Betws y Coed, The Conwy Falls Café and Restaurant is on the A5 near the junction with the B4406.

Public Transport: Buses from Llanrwst and Betws y Coed.

Start: Car park at the Conwy Falls Café and Restaurant. A charge may be made if not using the café.

Maps: Outdoor Leisure 17 and 18.

A turnstile to the right of the Conwy Falls Restaurant gives access to viewpoints of the Conwy Falls. Stained brown by journeying through peaty moorland, the river divides in two falling either side of a huge rock. A seventy yard manmade tunnel enables salmon to bypass the falls. The old salmon ladder on the rock was never used.

The Tea Shop

The Conwy Falls Café and Restaurant stands high above the rushing waterfalls. The varied menu includes light refreshments such as soup, bara brith, scones and teacakes. Open every day except Christmas Day, Monday to Friday 9am to 5pm, Saturday 9am to 9pm, and Sunday 9am to 6pm.

The Walk

1. From the car park walk out to the A5 and turn left. In about 200 metres descend a couple of steps on the left and follow a woodland path above the Conwy gorge.

Formerly a packhorse trail this track was improved to become a turnpike road on the London to Holyhead route in the early 19th century. However, it was very narrow and must have been dangerous for coaches. A few years later Thomas Telford built his great road higher along the hillside. It is now the A5.

2. After a ladder stile the path widens to a track. Keep ahead on this
track for nearly a mile until you reach a path on the left to the
Fairy Glen.

The romantic Victorians gave the dramatic ravine the name Fairy Glen. It
was a popular excursion from Betws y Coed.

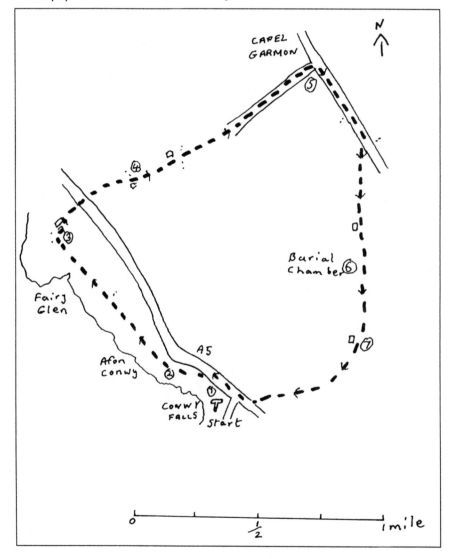

3. Go through a small gate on the right. Keep ahead through the field beside a fence on the left. Pass a house and bear left to a gate. Turn right uphill in the next field to the A5. Cross the road directly and at the bottom of a drive go through a gap in a high wall. Follow a clear path uphill with a wall on the right. In 200 metres the path leaves the wall to zigzag through trees and emerges on a forest track at a house called Ty'n y Bwlch.

4. Turn right and follow the track around a barrier and through a gate. The track curves left and becomes surfaced as it passes a cottage on the left. Go through a gate and continue past a farm to a lane junction near houses in Capel Garmon.

5. Turn right and pass a drive to Maes y Garnedd on the right. Continue uphill and cross a stile on the right. Follow the left fence and go through a kissing-gate. Continue to some farm buildings and go through a metal gate into a yard. Keep ahead to pass the farmhouse on the right and, where the drive turns left, bear right to a small gate at a post signed Capel Garmon Burial Chamber. Follow the right hand hedge and in 100 metres turn right through a metal gate. Cross the field to a kissing-gate in the fence surrounding the burial chamber.

Capel Garmon burial chamber

Capel Garmon burial chamber was built about 5000 years ago by Neolithic people. It is of a type found in the Cotswolds rather than Wales. Stones mark the extremities of the earth mound which once covered the tomb. There are three chambers but two have lost their capstones. During the 19th century it was used as a stable but since then some restoration work has taken place. Shards of Beaker pottery were found during excavations.

6. With the kissing-gate on your right keep ahead to a stile in a wall. Pass trees on your left and bear slightly left to a tall pole with an arrow. Go through a kissing-gate in a wall and go ahead through trees and a field to a footpath signpost. Bear right and follow the track ahead. Go through a gate and continue on the track to farm buildings at Penrhyddion Ucha.

7. Go through the farmyard and turn left on a surfaced track. In a few metres bear right to cross a stream and pass a building on your right. Go through a gate and cross the stream to another gate. Turn right and follow the right edge of the field downhill about 80 metres to a kissing-gate on the right. Cross the stream and bear left on a clear path through the trees to another kissing-gate. Continue to Rynys Camp Site and bear right to follow the access track through a gate. Descend to the A5 and turn right to the Conwy Falls Café and Restaurant.

11. Penmachno

Route: Ascending forest paths and tracks lead to fine views of the Conwy Valley and nearby mountains. The return is along a quiet lane above the tumbling afon Conwy and Machno Falls.

Distance: 3½ miles.

How to get there: Leave the A5 at the Conwy Falls Café and take the B4406 to the mill.

Public Transport: Buses from Betws y Coed and Llanrwst.

Start: Car park at the Penmachno Woollen Mill.

Maps: Outdoor Leisure 18.

The Penmachno Woollen Mill dates back from the 1830s when it was a fulling mill – a pandy – used by the local farmers. Cloth already woven on the farms was brought here to be finished under fulling hammers driven by a water wheel. The mill expanded to cover the whole process of carding, spinning and weaving.

The Tea Shop

Weavers Loft Café is in the Penmachno Woollen Mill buildings which date back to the 1830s. The menu includes soup, sandwiches, cakes and bara brith. There is a craft shop and you can watch the weaving process. The mill is open all year but the café closes for part of the winter. Otherwise it is open daily from 10am to 4.30pm. Tel: 01690 710545.

The Walk

1. From the car park walk out to the B4406. Turn left and in 25 metres turn left to pass the mill shop and cross a bridge over afon Machno. On your right there is a lovely old packhorse bridge. Although known as Roman Bridge it is probably medieval.

2. Continue along the lane and ignore a footpath signpost on the left. In another 100 metres turn left on a wide forest track lined with beech trees. Follow this track and in about 200 metres you will see the mill below on your left. Continue for another 50

metres and look for an old track on the right. (It is about 25 metres before the main track reaches a fork.) Follow the old track and go through a broad metal gate into a field. Keep ahead on a narrow path until you reach a track. Turn right to pass a house on the left.

The house is called Coed y Ffynnon – wood of the spring. This lovely building dates from the 16th century and a century later it was used as a nunnery. A medieval chapel once stood nearby and people came here to be cured by the healing waters at the chapel's well. It is said that a stone in the forest called maen sigla – shaking stone – always shook when the chapel's bell rang. The track ahead is Panorama Drive and it was constructed about 100 years ago when the house was used as a shooting lodge. Trees now screen the view and block the end of he drive.

3. Pass a field on the left and go through a gate into the forest. Con-

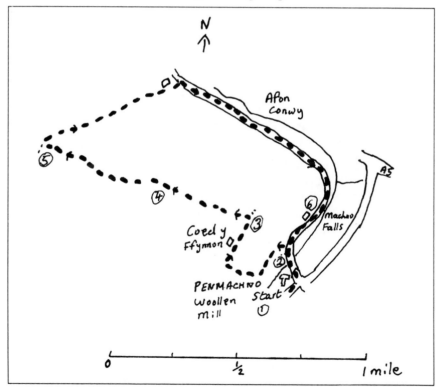

Coed y Ffynnon

tinue about 50 metres to some footpath waymarks. Turn left on a path uphill. When another path joins, continue uphill, following yellow paint marks where the path is indistinct and partially blocked by fallen trees. Eventually the path emerges on a grassy track. Turn left to reach a wide forest road near a large clearing where gravel is kept.

4. Turn right and follow the track as it swings left and gradually descends with fine views on the right of the Conwy Valley. Moel Siabod is prominent ahead and to its right are the Glyders, Tryfan and the Carneddau mountains. In just under a mile you will reach a junction of tracks. Where a track on the left goes uphill, look on your right for a less noticeable track.

This is a medieval track known as the path of Gruffydd ap Dafydd Goch. He lived at Fedw Deg high up on the hillside. A knight and related to Llywelyn the great, he fought in the French Wars for the Black Prince during the reign of Edward III. He was buried at St Michael's Church in Betws y Coed where there is a stone effigy of him.

5. Follow this overgrown track downhill. In just over half a mile the track passes behind cottages and reaches a lane. Turn right and

follow this quiet lane through mixed woods with afon Conwy rushing through a rocky ravine below on your left. In just under a mile there is a view of the confluence of the Conwy and Machno rivers. Continue 100 metres and look for a path on the left which leads to a viewpoint of the little known Machno Falls. Take great care here and do not let children or dogs rush ahead as there are steep cliffs with no fences.

6. Continue along the lane. In about 300 metres cross the bridge over afon Machno to return to Penmachno Woollen Mill and the start of the walk.

12. Dolwyddelan

Route: A fairly easy walk through fields and woodlands enjoying superb views with an opportunity to explore Dolwyddelan Castle.

Distance: 5 miles.

How to get there: Dolwyddelan is on the A470, off the A5 near Betws y Coed. In the village take the road signposted Dolwyddelan Railway Station to the car park.

Public Transport: Trains from Llandudno Junction to Blaenau Ffestiniog stop at Dolwyddelan if requested.

Start: Dolwyddelan car park at the railway station.

Maps: Outdoor Leisure 18.

Dolwyddelan, a small village in the lovely Lledr Valley, is named after St Gwyddelan who founded a church here in the 6th century. The Roman Road called Sarn Helen came through the valley on its way from Caerhun, near Conwy, to Carmarthen.

Dolwyddelan Castle in the lovely Lledr valley

The Tea Shop

The Tea Room is in the small Post Office opposite the road that leads to the car park at Dolwyddelan Railway Station. The menu offers hot and cold snacks including soup, beans on toast, toasted teacakes, sandwiches and scones. Open all year, Monday to Thursday 9am to 1pm and 2 to 5.30pm, Friday 9 to 1pm and Saturday 9 to 12.30pm. The tea room is also open Saturday and Sunday afternoons at bank holidays and during late July and August. Tel: 01690 750201.

The Walk

1. From the car park at the station walk out towards the school and turn left. At the road junction bear right to cross the bridge over afon Lledr and keep ahead past the church.

The church was built by local nobleman Maredudd ap Ieuan who took occupancy of Dolwyddelan Castle in the 15th century and later moved to a larger dwelling in Cwm Penamnen. It is believed he had twenty-six children! Because the old church on Bryn y Bedd was surrounded by thickets he feared ambush by outlaws and this was why he moved the church to the new site. The bandits had installed themselves in the old hospice of the Knights of St John at Ysbyty Ifan. When the knights abandoned the hospice the immunity they had been granted remained and no officer could enter the building to arrest the outlaws so they roamed and terrorised the neighbourhood.

2. At the A470, turn left and follow the pavement until you reach a small lay-by where the road crosses a narrow river, afon Ystumiau. Continue on the grass verge another 200 metres and just before reaching a house turn right through a gate onto a track. Pass farm buildings on the right and the house on the left. Follow the enclosed track through a gate to reach another track on a bend. The castle is ahead uphill. If you wish to see inside the keep take the track downhill to the ticket office. From the gate walk ahead uphill. In about 200 metres a path bears left to the castle.

Tradition claims that Dolwyddelan was the birthplace of Llywelyn ap Iorwerth, Llywelyn the Great. However, it is unlikely that he was born in this romantically situated castle because it is early 13th century. There was an earlier stronghold on the valley floor where he was probably born. The rectan-

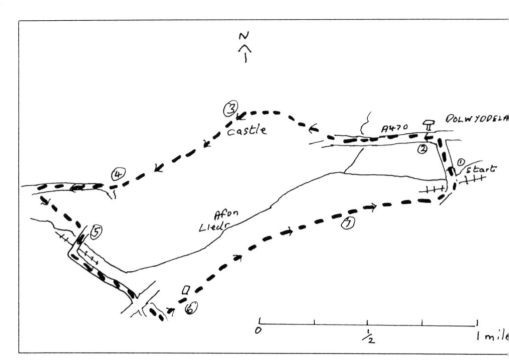

gular keep is thought to be the work of Llywelyn although the original building had only two storeys, a basement and a room with a fireplace. Maredudd ap Ieuan added another storey in the 15th century. Edward I captured the castle from Llywelyn's grandson, Llywelyn ap Gruffudd in 1283 and it is believed that the English built the second (west) tower. In the 19th century Lord Willougby de Eresby carried out some restoration work on the keep

3. To continue the walk, leave the main track where it bears right a few paces beyond the path to the castle. Turn left on a slightly sunken green track that passes below the towers. Continue ahead, shortly uphill, to a ladder stile. The track goes downhill to a gate. There are views of the mountain Moel Siabod on your right and the Lledr Valley ahead. Keep ahead to a walking man signpost on a rough track. Turn left and walk downhill to a lane.

4. Turn right on the lane for 500 metres. At a walking man signpost on the left, shortly before a farmhouse on the right, turn left through the field gate. Slant left downhill on a path marked by slabs of stone in places. At the end of the field go through a gap in

the wall and keep ahead to the next gate. Afon Lledr is now nearby on the right. Continue to a footbridge over a stream and follow a clear path to a small gate and lane.

5. Turn right to cross a bridge over afon Lledr. The lane continues over a railway bridge and bends left. Ignore a footpath signpost on the right. Follow the lane past the Roman Bridge railway station and reach the A470. Cross directly over the road to the lane opposite. In a few metres take a narrow path on the left. It goes alongside a stream and crosses a tributary stream. At an old slate bridge, cross the main stream and keep ahead through a gate and climb a ladder stile. Bear slightly right uphill following small posts with yellow arrows until you reach a track.

6. Turn left on the track and go through a gate. The right of way takes a slightly different route to the usual way at this point. Unless signs indicate otherwise bear slightly right to go through the farmyard, passing through two gates. After the second gate turn right alongside buildings. Cross a stream then bear left. Follow the track ahead to a gate which says private. Bear right here and walk uphill to another gate. Continue on a track and keep ahead through some woodland. In places stone slabs indicate the route across wet ground. The path bears left to cross a footbridge and a ladder stile.

7. Follow a fence on the left and then a wall on the right. In a few paces bear slightly right then immediately left to continue beside the wall. When the wall goes uphill keep ahead following posts with yellow arrows between outcrops of rock. Go downhill to a ladder stile. Pass a barn on your right and continue through gates, passing a house. Descend the access track. Other tracks join from the left and right. On reaching a road turn left. In about 40 metres turn left again to cross the railway line. The car park and the railway station are on the right. The tea room is ahead on the A470.

13. Beddgelert

Route: A superb walk in magnificent scenery with one long gradual climb through Cwm Bychan. The route starts by following the old railway track bed through the tunnels in the Aberglaslyn Pass. Torches are helpful but not essential.

Distance: 6 miles

How to get there: Beddgelert is south of Caernarfon at the junction of the A4085 and A498.

Public Transport: Buses from Porthmadog, Caernarfon and Llanberis.

Start: Car park on the A498, near the Royal Goat Hotel in Beddgelert.

Maps: Outdoor Leisure 17.

Beddgelert is a delightful small village lying deep in the mountains at the confluence of the rivers Glaslyn and Colwyn. The name Beddgelert means Gelert's Grave. Gelert was probably a saint who founded a monastery here. The legend of the dog Gelert stems from medieval folklore and, inspired by the popular story, the landlord of the Royal Goat Hotel made Gelert's grave in 1800 to promote tourism. Gelert was said to be a hunting hound of Prince Llywelyn. One day, returning from hunting, the prince found his dog covered with blood. Rushing to the nursery he saw that the cot was empty and, believing the dog had hurt his child, he killed Gelert with a sword. Too late his son started to cry and when Llywelyn found him he saw a dead wolf nearby. Gelert had killed the animal to save Llywelyn's son.

The Tea Shop

Lyn's Café and Tea Garden is near the bridge over afon Colwyn. The building has been a pub, police station, post office and bakery before becoming a café. The extensive menu includes breakfast, main meals, home-made pasta dishes, triple-decker sandwiches and cream teas. Sponge cakes, scones and specialities such as Snowdon Pudding are home-made. Open February to the end of October every day from 9am to 6pm. Holiday periods from 8am to 10pm. Tel; 01766 890 374.

The Walk

1. Walk out of the car park and turn left along the A498 to where the road turns left over a bridge.

On the right, on the corner of Church Street, stands Llywelyn's Cottage. The oldest house in the village, it may have been built on the site of Llywelyn's palace. This 16th century cottage was originally a farmhouse, later an inn and, in the early 20th century, accommodation for cyclists. The National Trust bought the building in 1985.

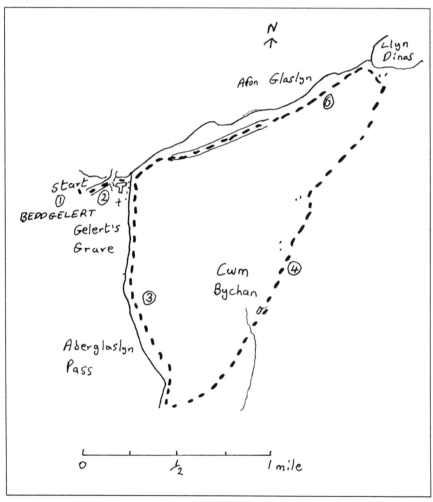

At the end of Church Street, St Mary's Church is usually open. This early Christian site became an Augustian Priory in the 13th century. It has been burnt down twice and most of the buildings were destroyed at the time of the dissolution of the monasteries. Only the chapel escaped destruction A triple lancet east window and two 12th century arches remain from the original chapel. Renovation work was carried out on the church in the mid-19th century. Under the old yew near the entrance to the churchyard there is a 17th century grave.

2. Do not cross the bridge but continue with afon Colwyn on your left. A few paces before a footbridge a path on the right leads to Gelert's Grave. If the Glaslyn Bridge is closed – see notices – return to this point to continue the walk. Cross the footbridge and turn right with afon Glaslyn on your right. Go through a kissing-gate and keep ahead. Pass an old railway bridge and keep ahead through the Aberglaslyn Pass.

The footpath is now on the track bed of the short-lived Welsh Highland Railway which ran between Caernarfon and Porthmadog. Opened in 1922, it closed fifteen years later. There are plans to reopen the line and if this happens the footpath will be diverted. With its high cliffs and tumbling river the dramatic scenery of the Aberglaslyn Pass has attracted tourists since the 18th century. Before the building of the Porthmadog embankment ships could sail to the entrance of the pass.

3. The pass narrows and the track goes through two small tunnels and a longer one. When you emerge from the long tunnel turn left uphill. The path climbs above a stream and, after passing a small waterfall, goes through a gate. Continue uphill through Cwm Bychan, crossing the stream by stepping stones and pass sheepfolds on your left.

Ascending Cwm Bychan you will see pylons from the old copper mine. Two cables ran between the pylons and the cable hoist used the weight of filled trucks to haul up the emptied ones. After two centuries of working the mine closed around 1930.

4. Ignore a left-hand path and climb towards a col on the skyline. Cross a ladder stile and in a few paces, at a fence, turn left to reach a footpath signpost. Bear right and descend the path to Llyn Dinas.

This beautiful lake was used for the shooting of the film 'Inn of the Sixth Happiness' starring Ingrid Bergman. During their perilous journey, whilst fleeing from the Japanese, the missionary and her schoolchildren crossed this end of the lake on a raft.

5. At the lake turn left over a ladder stile to have afon Glaslyn on your right. In 300 metres you will have a wooded hill on the opposite side of the river.

An Iron Age hill fort is on top of the wooded hill, which is called Dinas Emrys. According to legend, Vortigern built a castle here and after he fled to the Lleyn peninsula it was taken over by Merlin. It is said that in the fortress there is treasure buried by Merlin.

6. Continue to a bridge across the river. Do not cross but keep ahead, then bear left to reach the Sygun Copper Mine car park. Leave the track here and bear right to follow a wall on your right. Go through a gate and continue on a lane. When the lane bends right to cross a bridge, climb a stile on the left and continue through rhododendron bushes with the river on your right.

7. Pass the ruins of the Sygun corn mill. Continue through gates ignoring a bridge over the river. Keep ahead to cross the footbridge used earlier. The tea garden is on the left shortly before the road bridge in Beddgelert. Keep ahead to return to the car park.

Llyn Dinas

14. Blaenau Ffestiniog

Route: Probably the most strenuous route in this guidebook, this walk offers a mixture of moorland, mountain lake and riverside paths with spectacular views. Pick a clear day and be prepared for some rough and wet paths.

Distance: 8 miles.

How to get there: Blaenau Ffestiniog is on the A470 between Betws y Coed and Dolgellau.

Public Transport: Trains from Llandudno Junction. Buses from Dolgellau, Barmouth, Porthmadog and Caernarfon.

Start: Tourist Information Centre in Blaenau Ffestiniog. Car parks nearby.

Maps: Outdoor Leisure 18.

Although in the heart of Snowdonia, the town of Blaenau Ffestiniog is not included in the National Park. Nowadays dominated by the remains of slate quarries, two hundred years ago the head of the Ffestiniog Valley consisted of a few farms and pasture. Large scale quarrying began in the early 19th century and within a few years slate was being exported all over the world. By 1880 the population had grown to almost 12,000. The population is half that now and few are employed in the slate industry. Tours can be taken of the Llechwedd Caverns.

The Tea Shop

Myfanwy's is a friendly, small restaurant situated in Market Square at the bottom of Church Street. The varied menu includes grills, soup, jacket potatoes, omelettes, welsh rarebit, open sandwiches and cream teas. Open every day from noon to late evening. Tel: 01766 830059.

The Walk

1. With your back to the Tourist Information Centre, turn left to pass the Post Office on your right. Take the third street on your left. In about 20 metres, at Tai Llanddwyn, bear right up a narrow steep road. The road curves left and reaches a fork. Ignore the

road leaving on the right. Continue ahead and in another 50
metres bear right with the road to pass in front of houses. At the
end of the row turn left on a grassy path at a footpath signpost.
The path soon joins a fence on the right and follows it uphill to
join a track at a pink house.

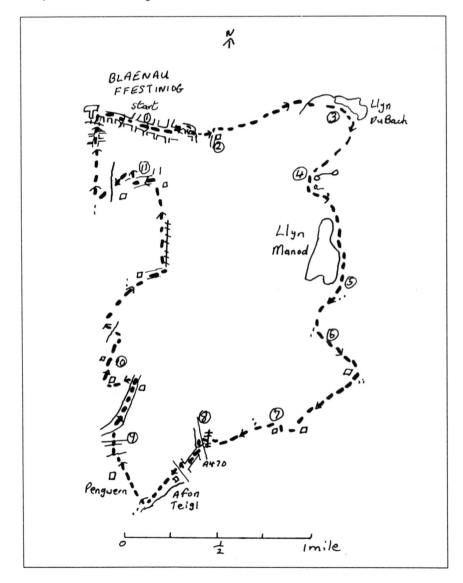

2. Turn left and in a few paces bear right through gates. Go ahead
    uphill and follow a fence beside a plantation. In a few paces leave
    this fence to head towards a fence corner on your left. Continue
    uphill and go through a gap between walls. Looking back there
    are fine views of the town and Moelwyn Mountains. The path
    bears to the right further away from the left-hand fence. Go
    through another gap in a wall and keep ahead. At a fork take the
    right-hand path which descends to pass the foot of a slate tip.
    The path rises again and crosses a stream. Continue on a narrow
    path uphill through heather and cross a stile in a fence. In about
    another 100 metres reach Llyn DuBach.

Above Llyn DuBach are the highest quarry workings in Wales. Graig Ddu
opened as an open cast quarry about 200 years ago and employed about
100 men, some living in barracks. This lake, which is actually two lakes was
constructed as a reservoir for the quarry.

3. The right of way goes over the hill to the right but a clearer path
    follows the lakeside. Keep the lake on your left until there is a
    wall across the lake. Here the path bears right, passing above the
    lake before continuing to a stile in a fence between walls. Llyn
    Manod, lying between Manod Mawr and Manod Bach, is now
    visible ahead. Bear right downhill on a path in the direction of
    the lake. Cross a bouldery section then pass a rocky hill on the
    left. The path passes between rocks and then a stream is below
    on the left. The path improves as it bears right and two small
    lakes, unnamed on the map, appear ahead. Continue between
    rocks and cross slates at the end of the lake.

4. Bear left to have the lakes on the left and pass the remains of a
    slate dressing mill. An incline from the Graig Ddu quarry de-
    scends the hill on your left. Pass the lakes and bear left uphill on
    a wide grassy path. In about 300 metres it curves right before
    reaching Llyn Manod. Ignore the kissing-gate on your right but
    keep ahead through a gateway to have the lake on your right.
    Continue along the foot of Manod Mawr's bouldery hillside.

During the Second World War pictures from the National Gallery were kept in
slate quarry caverns on the southern flank of Manod Mawr. The chambers
were kept at a warm temperature while housing the art treasures. Choughs
are often seen in this area.

5. At the end of the lake the path goes uphill and bears to the right.
    It soon levels and starts to descend. Ignore a path on the left.

The lonely cottage of Caecanol Mawr, with the Moelwyn mountains in the background

There are superb views ahead towards the sea, Trawsfynydd Lake and the Rhinog mountains. Descend parallel to a rocky hill on the left. The path becomes rather indistinct where it follows a fence on the right. After a rather wet section the way becomes clearer as it bears left going down to a small gate in a wall.

6. Continue on the clear path and cross a stile near a house with a large boulder in its garden Follow the track as it bears to the right and passes below the house. The track goes through a gate and passes a plantation on the right. Go through a gate before a farm and keep ahead above barns and the farmhouse. About 25 metres from the gate turn right at a fork and go uphill on a grassy track. At the entrance gate to a house, look for a small make-shift stile to the right of the gate. Cross it and walk between fences to a ladder stile.

7. Turn left to walk behind the house and continue on a green track. Ignore a right-hand fork. Passing a wall broken in places, descend to a ladder stile. Turn right to cross a stone slab over a stream then bear left uphill to some trees at an old railway track. Go through the gate and cross the bridge. Follow the track to the right and cross a ladder stile near a gate.

8. Cross the A470 carefully and turn left. In 50 metres turn right on a lane which narrows as it descends to a junction. Turn right and in 20 metres bear left through a small gate next to a larger one. Keep ahead on the path passing the old mill and walk alongside afon Teigl. Pass a number of small waterfalls and cross a couple of stiles. The path climbs away from the river before descending to a stile at a track. Turn right and go through a gate passing the drive to Pengwern on your left. Keep ahead and where the track bears right leave it to go through a gate ahead. Descend the field to have a wall on your left. Cross a small footbridge and go through a kissing-gate onto a lane.

9. Cross to another kissing-gate and walk ahead through the field to steps and a small gate. Turn right on the lane. In 650 metres, after passing farm buildings on the right, turn left on a track. Walk up-hill and pass a house on the right. Go through a gate and keep ahead on a drive. Before it bends left turn right through a kissing-gate. Follow the right-hand fence a few paces then slant left to descend through trees. Cross a wall at a corner and slant right to enter another field through a gap in a wall. Cross the field ahead to stone steps in a wall near two isolated trees.

10. Pass an old barn on the left. From here there are splendid views of the Moelwyn Mountains. Keep ahead through a gap in a wall and follow a path through another gap. Before the end of the next field the path bears left over a stream and emerges on a wide grassy path. Turn right and cross a stile at a gate. Follow the track through another gate onto an enclosed track. Keep ahead and go through a gate onto an access lane. Turn right and immediately after going through a gate turn left on a path to have a railway line on your right. The town of Blaenau Ffestiniog is in view ahead. Go through a kissing-gate and descend to a track. Keep ahead over a stile and in a few paces turn left on a farm access road.

11. In 200 metres cross a stile on the right and follow a clear path up-hill to reach the corner of a wall. Continue beside the wall for a few paces then take a path downhill to cross two footbridges. Keep ahead uphill to join a path below trees. Turn right uphill and join a road. Keep ahead to pass a supermarket and a park on the right. Continue in the same direction over an old hump-backed bridge that crosses the railway. Keep ahead to a square. Myfanwy's is on the left. On reaching Church Street turn right to the start.

15. Tanygrisiau

Route: This is a lovely, varied walk that starts by descending to waterfalls and woodlands along afon Goedol. A steep climb leads to remote Dduallt and a fine viewpoint. Dduallt Station on the Ffestiniog Railway is an alternative starting point.

Distance: 5 miles.

How to get there: Leave the A496 about one mile south of Blaenau Ffestiniog on the road signed Ffestiniog Power Station The car park is on the right in 250 metres.

Public Transport: Local bus from Blaenau Ffestiniog. The Ffestiniog Railway has a request stop at Tanygrisiau.

Start: Car park on the road leading to Ffestiniog Power Station.

Maps Outdoor Leisure 18.

The Tea Shop

The Butterchurn Lakeside Café is in the same building as the Ffestiniog Power Station Information Centre. Light meals are served including afternoon teas and home-made cakes. Open most of the year but check in the winter. Open Sunday to Friday 10am to 4pm. Tel: 01766 830950.

The Walk

1. From the car park turn left to the A496. Turn right on the grass verge and keep ahead passing an old cottage on the right. In another 30 metres turn left through a kissing-gate. Slant to the right uphill following stones marked with blue paint. In about 80 metres the path becomes clearer as it levels and then descends through bracken parallel to the road. When it reaches a track at a cattle grid bear right through a kissing-gate. In one of the corners of the grid there is a hedgehog ramp.

2. Turn right and in 50 metres turn left on a track that crosses a bridge at small waterfalls. Continue on the track and ignore a fork descending left. Pass a house on the right and where the track bears to the right take a path into the forest. Keep ahead

through the trees at varying distances from afon Goedol. The path goes through an area of moss covered boulders with ancient oak trees. In approximately another 150 metres it meets a path junction where a cottage is in view across a field to the right. Turn left to the river and left again to view the Goedol waterfalls. Return to the path and cross the ancient stone bridge over the river. Keep ahead between fields and where the track turns left go ahead through a small gate onto Woodland Trust land. In spring this path is bordered with a variety of flowers including primroses, wood sorrel and wood avens.

Waterfalls on afon Goedol

3. Follow the path to a track near a garage and turn right. The track passes through deciduous trees and climbs beside a field. Turn left through a kissing-gate and pass a barn on the left. Cross a stile near a bench. The mountains ahead are the Manods. The path bends to the left to pass under wires of pylons and goes through a kissing-gate. Follow a wall on the right to a fork. On your left there is a seat made in the shape of an oak leaf. Turn right to have a wall on the left and descend through oak trees. Cross a stile and descend to afon Goedol.

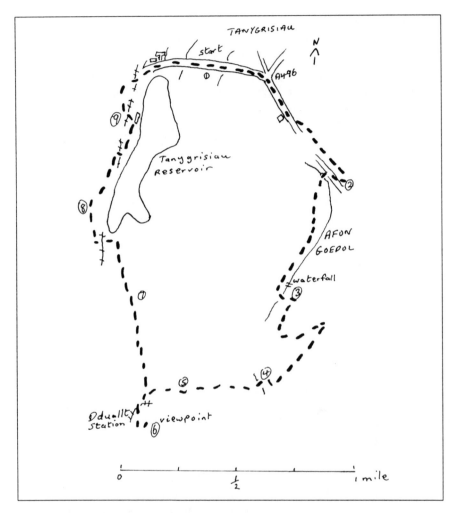

4. Turn right and follow a path to a footbridge. Cross the bridge and
follow the path as it bends to the left. In about 30 metres it curves
to the right steeply uphill. Cross a narrow stream on the left and
continue uphill through the forest. Some sections of the path are
quite rocky. At the edge of the forest, cross a ladder stile and keep
ahead through bracken to another stile on the right.

From this point onwards there is a chance of seeing feral goats, although
they do not allow people to approach very close to them. They are the de-

scendants of domesticated animals but have roamed free for many genera-
tions. There are several herds in Snowdonia. Mature billy goats have
magnificent horns.

5. Bear left on a track which goes uphill. It joins a track coming
   from a gate on the left. Turn right uphill beside a stream. At a fork
   turn left. Here a diversion can be made to Dduallt Station and
   viewpoint. Turn left in about 60 metres on a woodland path. Pass
   a pool on the left and cross a ladder stile. Go up to the old rail
   track bed and cross the Ffestiniog Railway line. Keep ahead
   along the platform.

On the station platform, there is a plaque to Colonel Andrew Campbell who
lived at Dduallt Manor when the Ffestiniog Railway was being restored. He
helped with the blasting necessary to construct the spiral. It goes around
the hill with the viewpoint before climbing the slope beyond the old station
master's house. The original line was drowned when the reservoir at
Tanygrisiau was built. The spiral was constructed to give more line for the ex-
tra gradient. At the end of the platform a stile on the left gives access to a
viewpoint of the surrounding mountains and countryside. A path on the
right-hand side of the track leads to Dduallt Manor which dates back over
400 years. It is said that Oliver Cromwell stayed there during the civil War.

6. Go back along the platform and cross the ladder stile to return to
   the track. Follow the track uphill to join the old railway track.
   Turn right along it and pass under a bridge. In another 100
   metres the track leaves the old line and bears left below the present Ffestiniog Railway. The old railway tunnel can be seen on the
   right.

7. The track goes uphill and in about 150 metres the Ffestiniog Railway enters a tunnel on your left. At a gate across the track there is
   a stone stile above on the left. Ahead are the Moelwyn Mountains
   and the Ffestiniog Power Station beside the reservoir. Descend
   the track and at a fork keep ahead a few paces then bear left to
   ladder stiles at the railway line. After crossing the line bear right
   uphill. The path crosses a stream and goes through gaps in walls.

The mine workings here are the remains of the Moelwyn Zinc Mine which operated about 100 years ago. The level stretch of ground was a tramway and
lower down, on the other side of the stream there are ruins of the mill com-
plex. On the opposite side of the lake, below the summit of the hill Moel

Ystradau, a granite quarry produced macadam and stone blocks for road making at the beginning of the 20th century.

When the reservoir is low the original Ffestiniog Railway track bed can be seen leading to the entrance of the old tunnel. The Queen opened the pumped storage scheme in 1963. Water released from Llyn Stwlan in a corrie below the Moelwyns drops 1000 feet whilst generating electricity. At night when demand is low the water is pumped back up to Llyn Stwlan. Tours of the Power Station can be booked at the Visitor Centre and it is possible to walk or drive up to Stwlan Dam. There is a charge for motorists.

8. Cross the footbridge and bear right on a path that descends to go through a short tunnel. At a fence bear left with the path to pass the mill site and descend gradually to a stile near a gate at the railway line. Cross the line and follow a track to the lakeside. Turn left to pass the remains of an old farmhouse which lost its land to the reservoir. When the track divides near a pylon take the left fork to a high fence. Follow a path that rises above the power station.

9. The path leads to the railway line and ladder stile. Continue over a footbridge and go uphill to a surfaced track and turn right downhill to cross the line again. At a road junction bear right to the lakeside and pass picnic tables on your left. Continue to the Ffestiniog Power Station Visitor Centre and the café. Continue along the road to return to the car park.

16. Tan y Bwlch

Route: This delightful woodland walk passes three lakes and climbs to superb viewpoints above the Ffestiniog Valley. The paths over Y Gysgfa (234m) are fairly steep but otherwise this is an easy walk on good tracks and paths. Some of the route follows courtesy paths which are closed on the 28th of February every year.

Distance: 5 miles.

How to get there: Leave the A487 5½ miles east of Porthmadog at the Oakley Arms. Follow the lane uphill and turn right before a railway bridge to Tan y Bwlch Station and café.

Public Transport: Take the Ffestiniog Railway from Porthmadog or Blaenau Ffestiniog to Tan y Bwlch. It operates from Easter to the end of October. Buses to the Oakley Arms from Caernarfon, Porthmadog, Blaenau Ffestiniog, Dolgellau and Barmouth.

Start: Car park at the Ffestiniog Railway Tan y Bwlch Station. There is also a small car park near Llyn Mair.

Maps: Outdoor Leisure 18.

The Ffestiniog Railway is possibly the most scenic narrow gauge railway in Wales. The line was first opened in 1836 to carry slate from Blaenau Ffestiniog quarries to the quay at Porthmadog. Trains descended by gravity and horses, which rode down with the slate, hauled the empty trains back to the quarries. In 1863 steam engines took over, amongst them the famous 'Prince' which is still working. Decline in the slate industry led to the line's closure in 1946 but eight years later it reopened and by 1958 trains were running again to Tan y Bwlch. After much hard work, mainly by volunteers, trains reached Blaenau Ffestiniog again in 1983.

The Tea Shop

Tan y Bwlch Café is alongside the Ffestiniog Railway station amongst lovely woodland scenery. Refreshments can be taken inside the café or outside at picnic tables. The menu includes light lunches and afternoon teas. Open daily from the last week in May to early September. Hours 10am to 4.30pm.

Steam locomotive at Tan y Bwlch

The Walk

1. With your back to the café walk ahead and turn right through a gate signposted 'Nature Trail'. On the immediate right there is a viewpoint of the woodlands.

Leaflets are available for the nature trail which descends through oak, birch, rowan and hazel. In spring look for violets, primroses, wild strawberries, celandine and cow-wheat. In deciduous woodland throughout the walk jays, pied flycatchers and woodpeckers may be seen or heard. On warm summer days butterflies, including the comma and green-veined white, flutter beside the paths. Look out, also, for dragonflies.

2. Return to the path and follow it downhill to a footbridge and road. Turn right and almost immediately go left through a gate to reach the picnic area at Llyn Mair. Ducks, coots and black-headed gulls are usually present 0n this tree-fringed lake.

3. With the lake on your left follow the broad track and cross a ladder stile beside a gate. Ignore a path on the left with open views of Llyn Mair in places. Continue to a fork. Turn right uphill and cross the Ffestiniog Railway line. Keep ahead to a track junction and turn right to Llyn Hafod y Llyn. A path descends to the

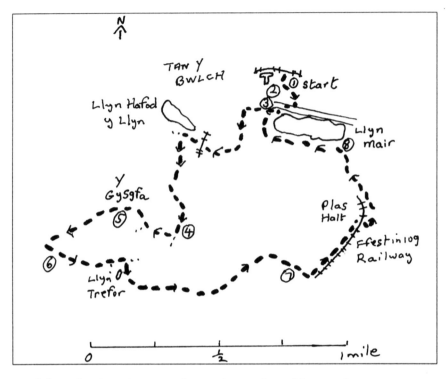

lakeside. Continue on the main track and in another 100 metres turn left on a track leading to an old building. Keep the building on your left and go ahead to a path. Turn right uphill and continue through woodland to a junction of paths.

4. Turn right uphill to a level area at a marker post (No. 32). Bear left – take care – on a path which ends above precipitous crags with fine views over the woodlands and Vale of Ffestiniog. Return to the marker post and keep uphill on the narrow path through heather, bilberry plants and conifers. The path rises to a cairn on the small summit of Y Gysgfa.

All around are magnificent views. To the north rise the Moelwyn Mountains, Cnicht, Snowdon and Moel Hebog. Harlech Castle lies south and to the west the Lleyn Peninsula.

5. From the cairn follow a narrow path in the direction of Harlech Castle. It descends into the conifers and becomes quite steep in places as it passes between bilberries and heather with fine

views of the estuary. The path broadens to a track and reaches a junction at post No. 33. Turn left and shortly reach an open stretch of hillside with lovely views of the Vale of Ffestiniog below.

During the last Ice Age the valley was gouged out by a huge glacier that flowed west from the mountains. It created a wide flat valley through which afon Dwyryd meanders eroding banks and dropping silt. Before the building of the Ffestiniog Railway slate was brought from the mountain quarries by horse and cart and loaded into quays along the river. The slate was then taken down the river to sea-going boats.

6. Continue along the track and bear right to pass Llyn Trefor on the right. Stay on this track until reaching post No. 6. At a left bend, turn right on another track and in 100 metres, where the track bends left, keep ahead on a narrow path with a low fence on the right. Cross ladder stile in a wall and keep ahead a few paces. Turn left on a narrow path. Shortly on the right there are fine views of the valley.

Further east, and below the railway line, stands the mansion of Tan y Bwlch, once home of the Oakeley family. In the late 18th century William Oakley from the Midlands married Margaret Griffiths, heiress of the Tan y Bwlch estate. He enlarged the house, rebuilt Maentwrog church across the valley and built earth embankments to prevent the river flooding. Shortly after his son inherited the estate, slate extraction began on Oakley land near Blaenau Ffestiniog, adding to the family's wealth. This influential family built a quarrymen's hospital in Blaenau Ffestiniog, village houses and a school in Maentwrog. They also landscaped the woodlands around the mansion with exotic trees, especially redwoods. The last Oakeley, Mary Inge, died in 1961. Plas Tan y Bwlch is now a residential centre for the Snowdonia National Park. Courses held there include walking, industrial archaeology and wildlife studies.

7. Follow the path to a small station (Plas Halt) on the Ffestiniog Railway. Cross the line and follow the zigzags to a fairly level path. Turn left to reach a broad track at post 12. Bear left and pass a pool on the right. The track descends and when it bears right keep ahead in the direction of a seat above Llyn Mair.

8. Follow the path alongside the lake. In early summer there are water lilies here. The path goes through a wall and joins the track walked earlier. Turn right to the road. Turn right then left and take one of the Nature Trail paths to the station, car park and café.

17. Porthmadog

Route: A lovely walk that crosses the shoulder of Moel-y-Gest, Porthmadog's own mountain. There are superb views along the route.

Distance: 7½ miles.

How to get there: Porthmadog is on the A497, south of Caernarfon.

Public Transport: Trains on the Machynlleth-Pwllheli line stop at Porthmadog. Buses from Caernarfon, Blaenau Ffestiniog and nearby towns and villages.

Start: Edinburgh Woollen Mill Shop near the traffic lights at the south-east end of Porthmadog. Car parks nearby.

Maps: Outdoor Leisure 18. A short section of the walk is off the 1998 edition of the map but if the directions are followed carefully there should not be any problems.

Before the 1880s, Porthmadog did not exist. Early in the 19th century, William Alexander Madocks reclaimed seven thousand acres of land from the sea by building the mile long embankment across the

Porthmadog harbour

Glaslyn estuary. By 1826, the new harbour was completed and ten years later the Ffestiniog Railway opened bringing slates from Blaenau Ffestiniog quarries to the waiting ships. In the estuary there is an island, known as Cei Ballast, which was formed from the ballast thrown off ships coming into the harbour to load. Slates were exported to roof houses all over the world, including Australia.

The Tea Shops

From an abundance of refreshment places I have included a coffee shop half-way and two in Porthmadog. **Tyn Llan Coffee Shop** is in old farm buildings that have also been converted into a craft shop and small museum. Hot snacks, sandwiches and home-made scones are served in the former stable. Open Easter to October 10am to 6pm. Closed on Sundays at the beginning and end of the season. Tel: 01766 512175. **The Bowsprit Café** in Cornhill has outdoor tables from where it is possible to enjoy the activity around Porthmadog harbour. Hot and cold snacks are available. Open Easter to October from 8.30am until late afternoon or evening, according to the weather. **Yr Wylan** in the High Street is a cosy restaurant and the varied menu includes hot meals, salads and afternoon teas. Open Easter to October daily from 10am to 6pm. Shorter opening hours in the winter. Tel: 01766 513188.

The Walk

1. With your back to the Edinburgh Woollen Mill Shop, cross the A497 at the traffic lights and turn right. Cross the bridge over afon Glaslyn and, opposite the Ffestiniog Railway Station, turn left. Pass Cob Records on the right and at a fork in the track go left. Keep ahead over the sluice gates and continue on a tarmac path beside Llyn Bach. When the path joins a road turn left.

2. In approximately 100 metres turn right and take a narrow path to the right of the Car and Motorcycle Museum. Cross two stiles – take care – at the railway line and keep ahead through a kissing-gate. Join a track and continue with the Welsh Highland Railway line on the left. Pass Pen y Mount Station and go through a kissing-gate. Turn left and follow the lane to the A487.

3. Bear right, taking care, for 100 metres and at a stone stile on the

right enter woodlands. Keep ahead on a track and, in about 30 metres, turn right on a narrow path. In a few paces it bears left using planks to cross wet patches of ground. Follow the path as it climbs left and soon levels passing below cliffs. Reach a wider track and turn left to have a field on the right. Ignore a track on the left. Keep ahead to the A487 at Tremadog.

Tremadog dates from the early 19th century when W.A. Madocks intended it to be a town on the coach route from London to Ireland. Built on reclaimed land, it is a fine example of early town planning with its market square, coaching inn and town hall. Porth Dinllaen on the Lleyn Peninsula was the intended port for the Irish Mail but, in the end, the government preferred Holyhead. T.E. Lawrence (Lawrence of Arabia) was born here in 1888.

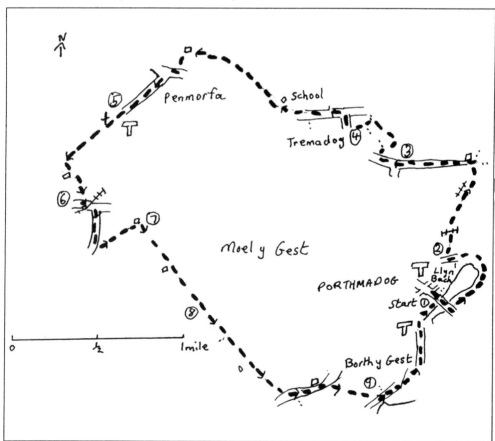

4. Bear right and at a road junction turn left to pass the Madog Hotel
   on the right. In approximately 300 metres pass a road sign for
   Caernarfon and in another 50 metres turn right on a road. Pass a
   school and keep ahead through a kissing-gate. Follow the green
   enclosed track to a small gate into woodland. Go ahead on a track
   and follow it to a kissing-gate. Walk along an embankment to another kissing-gate and keep ahead. Just after a house join a track
   and immediately turn left on an enclosed path downhill. At a
   track bear right to the A487 at Penmorfa. Turn right and in a few
   metres bear left on a lane which descends and rises again to Tyn
   Llan Craft Museum and Coffee Shop.

For many centuries this lane was a main road on the pilgrimage route to
Bardsey Island. Drovers leaving the Lleyn Peninsula with their sheep, cattle
and geese waited at Tyn Llan for low tide before crossing the tidal marshes.
The church dates from the 14th century. It has a memorial to Sir John Owen a
Royalist leader during the Civil War who was condemned to death by the Par-
liamentarians. He secured a reprieve and lived to see the restoration of
Charles II.

5. Ignore a track on the left and keep ahead to pass cottages and the
   church. Go through a gate across the track and keep ahead to go
   through another gate at footpath signposts. Turn left at the sign
   for Borth y Gest and enter a gate. Follow a wall and cross a
   stream. Pass a cottage and keep ahead to a gate. Keep ahead
   through rhododendrons. Walk past a cottage and, just before a
   garage, turn right on a track to reach the A497.

6. Turn left under a bridge and immediately turn right on a wooded
   lane. Follow it for 700 metres. After passing a footpath on the
   right turn left on a track at a footpath signpost. In a few paces
   leave the track at a low yellow arrow to take a path through trees.
   Pass a wall on the right and cross a track. Keep ahead into a field
   and walk beside the right boundary to a small gate. Go uphill on a
   path and continue ahead to meet a track running alongside a
   fence.

7. Turn right to have fine views of the coastline. Pass a plantation
   on the left and reach a pair of gates. Go through the left gate and
   pass above a house called Bron y Foel. Go through another gate
   and keep ahead beside a broken wall on the left. (The small gate

seen across the left-hand field gives access to a steep path that reaches the summit of Moel y Gest.)

8. Cross a ladder stile to the right of a gate and bear left a few paces to follow an old track alongside a broken wall. Descend through gorse and cross a stream at a gate. Keep ahead to pass a pool on the right and cross a ladder stile at a road. Cross the road carefully and turn left. Ignore the footpath on the immediate right. Follow the grass verge for 450 metres and, opposite a gate to a house on the left, turn right along a track with a signpost for Borth y Gest. Go through a gap beside the gate ahead and follow the wall to a kissing-gate. Continue on a clear path through woodland. Pass through a small gate and cross a field to another path. Descend beside houses to the sea front at Borth y Gest.

Borth y Gest is older than Porthmadog and two hundred years ago was a regular haunt of smugglers. Small boats were built here. It is said that in the 12th century Prince Madoc sailed from here and discovered America far earlier than Columbus. The beach is rather muddy but, to the right and beyond a car park, a cliff top path gives access to small sandy coves.

9. Turn left and at the end of the sea wall bear right to follow a low wall above a short stretch of shingle beach. Go up steps to join a road but where it bends left, keep ahead to a footpath signpost. Follow the track that descends to a level area. Keep ahead to pass boatyards and reach the Bowsprit Café near the quayside. Follow the edge of the quays passing Porthmadog Maritime Museum. Continue to the main road and turn left to the start, Yr Wylan and car parks.

18. Bala

Route: A lovely varied walk that follows riverside paths before climbing a wooded hillside with superb viewpoints above Bala Lake.

Distance: 4¾ miles.

How to get there: Bala is on the A494. Leave the A5 west of Corwen.

Public Transport: Buses from Dolgellau and Wrexham.

Start: Car park near the bridge on the A494 at the north-east end of Bala.

Maps: Outdoor Leisure 18.

Bala is an attractive small market town lying at the eastern end of the lake with the same name. Its long main street follows the line of the Roman Road from Chester to a fort at Caer Gai, slightly south-west of Bala Lake. The town and surrounding area used to be famous for its knitted stockings. In the High Street there is an impressive statue to Thomas Ellis, the Liberal MP for Meirionnydd in 1886. He became Chief Whip in 1894. In Tegid Street there is a statue to Rev Thomas Charles from whom the famous Mary Jones bought a Bible in 1800 after walking barefoot from Abergynolwyn.

Bala town and lake

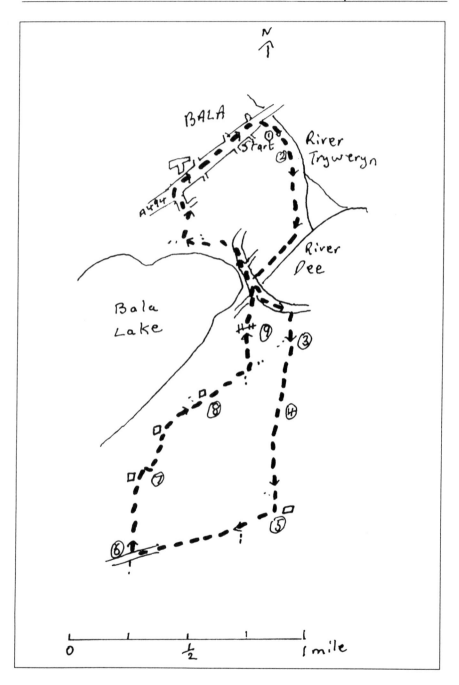

The Tea Shop

Y Radell is an old building dating back about 400 years. There is a collection of old farming implements, some on the walls. Hot meals and afternoon teas, including home-made cakes are on the menu. Open all year 9am to 5pm. Tel: 01678 520203.

The Walk

1. Leave the car park by taking the track through pines to an embankment. Turn right along the River Tryweryn. Go through a gate and keep ahead.

The River Tryweryn flows from Llyn Celyn a reservoir which was created to provide water for Liverpool. The Tryweryn joins the Dee in just over half a mile.

2. Shortly after a weir turn right through a gate, cross a track to a smaller gate and continue to another weir. The embankment bears right and soon follows the River Dee. You may see ducks, herons and swans. Continue to a kissing-gate at a road. Turn left and cross the bridge over the Dee. Bear left with the road and pass a campsite on the right. At the end of the site turn right on a track that is a bridleway.

3. In about 100 metres turn left at a walking man sign on a clear path that climbs through oak and birch trees. When it joins a track continue uphill to meet a wide forest track at a footpath signpost. Turn left but in a few paces bear left off the track onto a path going uphill. Cross a wide grassy track and keep ahead to a stile at the edge of the forest. Keep ahead uphill to a fence. Bear right alongside the fence and at a corner turn left uphill to a stile. Look back for superb views of Bala Lake and town.

Although only four miles in length, Bala Lake is the largest natural lake in Wales. The Welsh name is Llyn Tegid and many legends are attached to the lake. It is said that a cruel prince ruled the area and that during a feast the palace and surrounding area were drowned. The only survivor was a local harpist who had been forced to provide entertainment at the court. While he was playing he became aware of a small bird voicing the word 'vengeance' and he followed the bird out of the palace and high into the mountains. At daybreak when he looked back he saw the inundation. Another legend tells of how a guard neglected to replace the cover on a spring and the valley and town disappeared under the flood of water.

Many varieties of bird visit the lake including heron, duck and waders. Species of fish include the gwyniad which has been trapped in this lake since the last Ice Age. It is found nowhere else in Britain.

4. Cross the stile and slant right to a corner stile near a gate. Follow the fence to a stile in a corner. Go ahead uphill, at first through gorse, and continue on a clear path that crosses a grassy track. Keep ahead and walk towards a house. Before reaching the house cross a stile in a fence and continue on a rough track.

5. Turn right on the track and at a fork keep right. Ignore a footpath on the left and continue with fine views of Bala Lake. At another track turn right in the direction of the lake and bear left through a gate. Keep ahead on the lane as it descends to cross a cattle grid. Continue with a fence on the left, which soon bears away uphill. In another 30 metres turn right on a path.

6. Follow the path in the direction of a fence. In about 100 metres continue parallel with this fence. When the fence bears away to the right continue to descend in the direction of Bala and a nearer house across a field. Cross a stile in a corner and follow the fence on your left. Pass the house on your left.

7. After crossing a stream, which goes below the path, bear right uphill to a fence corner. Turn left alongside the fence and pass above a farm. Keep close to the fence and reach a stile in a corner. Go ahead, descending slightly to a green path between trees and bushes and when it descends to a track turn right.

8. At a fork in the track walk between buildings. Keep ahead to pass a car park. Ignore a track on the right that goes uphill. Pass a ruin and farm buildings on the left. Ignore a footpath on the right and, in another 40 metres, cross a rough stile next to a gate on the left. Follow the left fence to another stile and keep ahead bearing slightly right to a wooden kissing-gate. Cross the bridge over the Bala Lake Railway line.

The narrow gauge railway runs from this station to Llanuwchllyn just beyond the southern end of Bala Lake. The line has been laid along the trackbed of the Ruabon to Barmouth line which closed in 1965.

9. Pass the little station and follow a path to the road. Cross to an old bridge and keep ahead over the main bridge crossing the River Dee. Continue to a fork and turn left. At a right bend in the road turn left through a kissing-gate to take a path along the embankment. Ignore a path on the right to a kissing-gate but keep ahead another 200 metres to a kissing-gate into a field. You may wish to continue along the embankment to see more of the lake before returning to Bala from this point. In the field follow the left fence and go through a gate onto an enclosed path. Keep ahead to a road and turn left. Pass a parking area and go ahead to meet crossroads on the A494. Turn right into Bala town centre. The tea room, Y Radell, is on the left in about 100 metres. Continuing along the street you will reach the car park.

19. Harlech

Route: Ascending paths with magnificent views of mountains and coast are followed by a stroll along the sands. If possible check tide times as a short section of beach may be impassable for a while when the tide is in.

Distance: 6 miles.

How to get there: Harlech is off the A496 north of Barmouth.

Public Transport: Trains on the Cambrian Coast line stop at Harlech. Buses from Barmouth and Blaenau Ffestiniog.

Start: Car park near the bus stop in upper Harlech.

Maps: Outdoor Leisure 18.

Harlech is a charming small hillside town built around King Edward I's fortress on its promontory rock. The castle is one of a chain built in the 13th century to subdue the Welsh. It took only seven years to build and the architect, Master James of St George, became the first constable. At that time the sea came in as far as the rock and supplies

Harlech castle

were brought to the garrison by ship. However, Owain Glyndwr took the castle in 1404 and it became his residence for approximately four years until sieged by the English. The strong Lancastrian resistance during the Wars of the Roses originated the song 'Men of Harlech'. During the Civil War it was the last castle to be taken by the Parliamentarians.

The Tea Shop

Plas Café dates back to the 17th century when it was owned by an important local family, the Nannaus. Meals can be taken on the terrace while enjoying wonderful coastal views. Hot meals and afternoon teas are available with a delicious selection of cakes. Open most of the year but closed part of the winter. Usually open from mid February onwards. Open from 9am to 5pm (4.30pm in the winter). Open evenings in the summer. Tel: 01766 780204.

The Walk

1. From the car park walk down to the main street and turn right. Pass the Tourist Information Centre and Plas Café on the left. Pass the Midland Bank and take the next turning right. Walk uphill and shortly turn left on a narrow lane to have fine views of the castle. At another lane near a cemetery turn left. Ignore a footpath going downhill. Continue ahead for about 100 metres and then turn left on an enclosed path.

2. Follow the path above houses and through trees. Cross over a lane and keep ahead passing a house. Go through two gates and in a few paces turn right uphill. Follow a wall on the right and, about 25 metres before reaching a farmyard, turn left. Walk above your earlier path so as to have a rocky hillside on the right. In 100 metres at waymarks on a small tree bear right uphill and follow a wall to a stone stile. Continue uphill through gorse and hawthorn to join another path and turn right. At a point where telephone poles cross the path look for a marker post. Here take a path uphill between bracken and gorse to a kissing-gate. Turn right on an access lane to have superb coastal views.

3. On reaching a lane junction turn right downhill for 100 metres. Turn left through a gate at a footpath signpost. Pass a house on

the right and go through a gate. Take the second gate on the right onto an enclosed track. Emerge in an open field and bear left uphill. After walking between walls go through a gap into another field. Bear right on a path above a wall. In about 120 metres slant left to a tall marker post near a wall. Go over a stile in the wall and cross a narrow field to a lane.

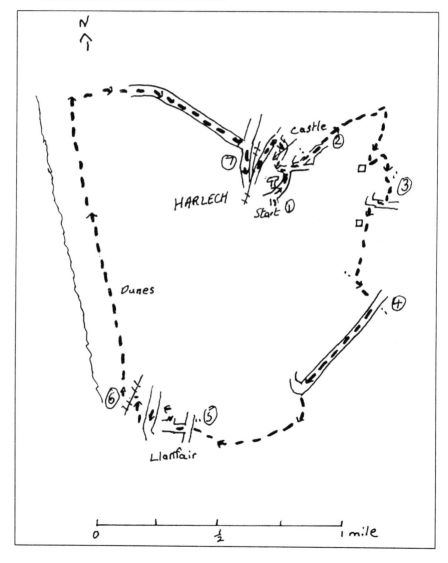

4. Turn right on the lane to have superb views of the Rhinog Mountains. In 600 metres ignore a footpath signpost on the right. Continue to where the lane bends right and turn left through a gate next to a cattle grid. Walk ahead about 10 metres then slant right on a clear path between gorse and bracken. Go through a gate into a field and bear right downhill. Cross a stone stile to the left of a gate. Keep ahead following a wall and go through a gate onto an enclosed track. Continue with a wall on the right. Pass a house on the left and go through a gate onto a lane near the village of Llanfair.

5. Turn right and at a lane junction cross directly over the road. Keep ahead and in about 80 metres turn right on a wide track between houses. Descend steps to the A496. Cross carefully and turn left. At a left bend in the road turn right through a kissing gate onto National Trust land. There is a seat here with fine views of Harlech beach. Follow a path to a kissing-gate. Continue on an enclosed path and in 30 metres go through another gate to descend steps to a railway line. Cross with care and go over a wooden bar stile. Steps go down to the beach.

6. Bear right along the beach. In just over a mile reach a section where there is a fence bordering the sand dunes. At a wide gap in the fence turn right to follow a sandy path to a car park. Take the road ahead to the A496.

7. Turn right and go over the level crossing. Immediately turn left on a lane below Harlech Castle. Pass a caravan park on the right and at its end turn right on a lane uphill. Near children's swings walk towards the castle then bear left to pass the Castle Hotel. Turn left to the main street and bear right to Plas Café and the start.

20. Tal y Bont

Route: An interesting, lovely walk that starts by following a woodland path beside a tumbling river. The route passes a Neolithic burial chamber and there are spectacular views.

Distance: 4½ miles.

How to get there: Tal y Bont is on the A496 north of Barmouth.

Public Transport: Buses from Barmouth, Harlech and Blaenau Ffestiniog.

Start: Car park near the Ysgethin Inn at Tal y Bont.

Maps: Outdoor Leisure 18.

The Tea Shop

The Ysgethin Café is in the same building as a rural life museum. Hot food is available and afternoon teas. Open most of the year but check in the late autumn and winter. Open Monday to Saturday 9am to 5pm. Tel: 01341 247141.

Cors y Gedol burial chamber (see point 2)

The Walk

1. From the car park pass the Ysgethin Inn on the right and take a path between a building and a fence. Reach the River Ysgethin and continue through a small gate. Keep the river on your right and stay on the main path as it climbs through beautiful broad-leaved woods. At a fork near a seat bear right and follow the path until you reach a lane near a cottage.

The cottage, which is called Llety Lloegr (English Shelter) used to be an overnight stop and a shoeing station for drovers, For hundreds of years, and well into the 19th century, Welsh Black Cattle were driven to English markets. Cattle were shod for the journey and on their hoofs they wore two pieces of narrow metal.

2. If you divert downhill for about 100 metres you will see an old bridge called Pont Fadog. A stone on the bridge bears the date 1762. Return to the cottage and follow the lane to a burial chamber on the left.

Cors y Gedol Neolithic burial chamber is also known as Arthur's Quoit. The tomb has a large capstone and two upright stones. According to local legend King Arthur threw the capstone from the top of the rounded hill called Moelfre.

3. Continue on the lane and go through a gate. Turn left for 200 metres and, at a corner, keep ahead on a track which bears right to a gate. The old mansion to the left is Gors y Gedol. Follow a wall on the left and go through another gate. Keep ahead and climb a stone stile in a corner. Go right about 30 metres, then bear left on a path which crosses a stream.

4. Follow a stony path through gorse and go through a gate. Continue with a wall on the left. When the wall bends left, go through a gap in another wall and follow the path to a footpath signpost near a lane. There are fine views of the high hill Moelfre to your right.

5. Turn left on the lane through open fields and pass riding stable buildings. Go through a gate across the lane and in 15 metres turn left through a gate at a bridleway sign.

6. Follow a path through a gap in a wall. Keep ahead through scat-

tered trees and woodland. Climb some steps into a field and keep
ahead to a lane. Cross the lane and climb steps in a wall beside a
house called Parc Uchaf. Keep ahead through two narrow fields
via gates. There are wonderful views of the coast at this point.
Keep ahead and aim for the right-hand corner of the next field
where fences meet at a wood.

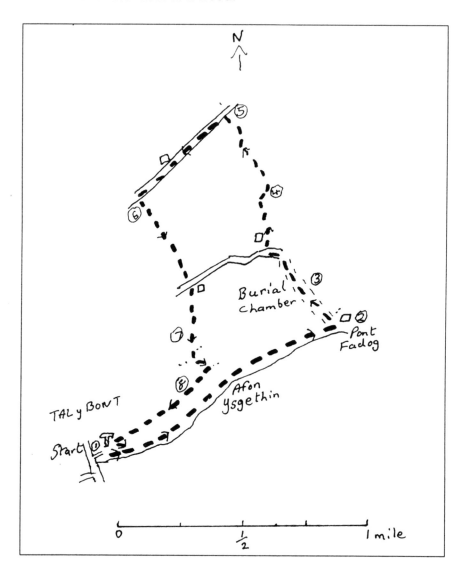

7. Go through a gate and keep ahead with broad-leaved trees on the left and a fence on the right. When the fence bends right at a junction join a track on the left to continue ahead. Ignore a right-hand track but keep ahead on the main track, which becomes very wide between low walls. At a track junction turn right to descend above the riverside path used earlier.

8. Go through a gate and walk alongside a fence, which is on your right. Pass a small field. Join an access track and keep ahead downhill passing bungalows on the right. When the track meets a road, immediately turn left on a footpath. Go through a gap in a wall and follow the path to the River Ysgethin. Bear right and retrace your steps through the small gate to reach the entrance gates to the café and museum.

21. Dolgellau

Route: A varied walk with some climbing and fine views on the descent. A stream crossing may present problems after heavy or prolonged rain. An alternative route is given in the directions.

Distance: 4½ miles.

How to get there: Dolgellau is north of Machynlleth, at the junction of the A470 and A494.

Public Transport: Buses from Tywyn, Barmouth, Machynlleth, Wrexham and Blaenau Ffestiniog.

Start: Car park near the bridge across afon Wnion.

Maps: Outdoor Leisure 23.

Backed by the mountain range of Cader Idris, Dolgellau is an attractive small town on the banks of afon Wnion. The town grew around the woollen industry when the majority of the cottagers were involved in spinning and weaving. Most streams had several fulling mills where the cloth was finished before export, some to America.

Y Sospan tea room in Dolgellau

Dolgellau has many historic buildings. The bridge near the car park was built in 1638. St Mary's Church near the square dates from 1716. Inside there is a 14th century carved effigy.

The Tea Shop

Y Sospan Tea Room and Restaurant dates from 1606. The building was formerly the Town Hall with lock-ups and a courtroom. The menu includes hot meals, pizzas, toasties and pastries. Open all year but closed on Sundays. Hours 9am to 5pm (closes 4.30pm in the winter). Tel: 01341 423174.

The Walk

1. From the car park follow the direction of the large walking man sign and walk through a passageway to a lane. Turn right, then first left, and pass Y Sospan on your right. Keep ahead through Eldon Square. At the end of the square bear left and follow the road as it curves to the right and crosses the bridge over the River Arran.

2. Immediately bear right to follow the river on your right. On reaching a road keep ahead and at its end continue uphill to a walking man sign on a lamp-post. Take the right-hand surfaced track uphill. After the last house the track becomes grassy with open views over the Arran Valley and back towards Dolgellau. Look for a stile on the right. (If the weather is wet and you wish to avoid the stream continue on the track to a lane and turn right to join the main route at direction 4).

3. Cross the stile and walk ahead, downhill to a path which runs above trees and the river. Pass a weir and cross a footbridge over the Arran. Follow a track but do not cross a bridge on your right. Turn left over a stile and continue beside a fence. The path passes through woods to have the river below on the left. It climbs a few steps and in about 150 metres descends slightly to a ladder stile. Cross a stream at stepping stones. Continue on a woodland path and cross a footbridge over the river. Pass a building to reach a wider track and then a lane.

4. Turn right on the lane uphill above the rushing afon Arran.. In 600 metres turn left through a gate with the names Yyddyn

Ednnyfed and Dref Gerig. Follow the surfaced track through fields and woodland. Ignore the left fork and go through a gate at the edge of the forest. In 50 metres turn right on a clear path along the hillside. Go through a gap in a wall into coniferous trees. Pass a ruin and keep ahead through the trees to a lane.

5. Turn left and in about 20 metres turn right through a gate. Keep ahead to cross a footbridge. Bear right on a wide track. In approximately 80 metres ignore a footpath signpost. Keep ahead descending the track and in another 60 metres go through a gap in a

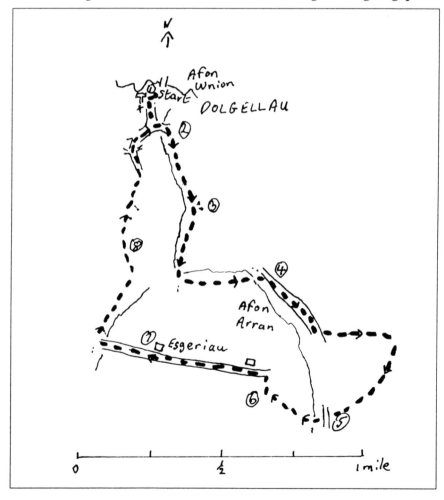

wall where there was once a gate. Immediately turn left to cross a stile. Slant slightly right as you keep ahead through oak and birch trees, keeping a wall at varying distances on your left. In 200 metres the path reaches a fork. Take the left fork and follow a wall to a stile on your left.

6. Cross the stile and descend steps to a track. Turn right and at a lane bear left to pass Parc Cottage. Follow the lane uphill to pass a cottage called Esgeriau on your right and reach a track to Bryn Mawr on your left.

Bryn Mawr was the home of Rowland Ellis who became a Quaker in 1672. George Fox had visited the area in 1657 and many local farmers and gentry were converted after hearing his message that man could reach God directly without the church hierarchies or rites. Quakers would not swear any kind of oath and this led to persecution after the restoration of Charles 11. Several Quakers were imprisoned because they would not take the oath of Allegiance. Rowland Ellis and others were taken to court in Bala and Judge Walcott told them they were traitors and should be hanged, drawn and quartered and the women burnt. Fortunately a London lawyer was able to prove that the law had already been repealed and the prisoners were set free. William Penn acquired land for the Quakers in America and this became Pennsylvania. Many Welsh Quakers emigrated including Rowland Ellis. He gave his new farm the name Bryn Mawr which was the name of his home here near Dolgellau. Later this name was given to a well-known women's college there.

7. Continue on the lane, which descends to a stream at a footpath signpost. Turn right to follow the bridleway. Ahead are fine views of the Rhinog Mountains and to the east are Y Garn, Diffwys and the Arans. Looking back you will see Cader Idris. Stay on the main track which rises over the side of a hill. Before reaching a wall bear right and descend to a gate.

8. Follow an enclosed track downhill. Ignore a footpath into a field. Bear left to a footpath signpost at a house. Turn right downhill and at a fork go left. At a junction of lanes keep ahead along Love Lane (Tylau Mair). On reaching the next road turn right and follow it to Eldon Square. The Information Centre at Ty Meirion has a Quaker exhibition Retrace your steps to Y Sospan and the car park

22. Barmouth

Route: A short walk that starts with ascending paths on the hillside above Barmouth. There are wonderful views throughout the walk.

Distance: 3½ miles.

How to get there: Barmouth is on the A496, west of Dolgellau.

Public Transport: Trains on the Machynlleth – Pwllheli line stop at Barmouth. Buses from Bala, Dolgellau, Harlech and Blaenau Ffestiniog.

Start: Barmouth Railway Station. There are several car parks nearby.

Maps: Outdoor Leisure 23.

Barmouth grew as a holiday resort in the 19th century when sea bathing became fashionable. To cater for the visitors shops, houses and hotels were built on the flat sands, an area once covered by tides.

The earlier houses of the town had been built in tiers on narrow ledges against the hillside. Before the coming of the railway, shipbuilding was a major industry at the harbour and in the many creeks of the Mawddach. Barmouth Bridge has a swing section to permit the passing of ships. Timber and oak bark were early exports followed by coarse cloth woven at Dolgellau. Ty Crwn, the Round House on the quay was built in 1830 as a lock-up for drunks who had become a nuisance on the streets. In Ty Gwyn a medieval building nearby conspiracies took place against Richard III.

The Tea Shop

The Old Tea-rooms occupy an early 18th century building. An extensive menu ranges from main meals, jacket potatoes and salads to sandwiches and cream teas. In the Summer open six days a week. Closed on Wednesdays all year. From 1st November to Easter open Thursday, Friday, Saturday and Sunday. Hours 10.30am to 5pm. Tel: 01341 280194.

The Walk

1. From Barmouth Railway Station go over the level crossing and keep ahead to the A496. Cross the road and walk along Water

Street. The road bears right and meets another lane on the left called Tan y Graig. Go steeply uphill and at a fork bear left. In another 30 metres turn left at a footpath signpost below tall houses.

2. Go through a gate across the path and ignore a gate on the left. Continue uphill and follow the track, passing an old mine entrance. The track bends right to a fork. Ignore the grassy track ahead and bear left. Pass a ruin and go through a gate. Follow he track to a ruined barn at the old farm of Cell-fechan. Do not bear right with the track. At the end of the barn turn left through a gap in the wall and slant right to another gap and a small gate. Turn left up the heather hillside to a cairn on the small peak of Craig y Gigfran. On the north facing side of the hill there is a plaque to soldiers from Birmingham. Take care here as there is a steep drop. On a clear day, views stretch to the Lleyn Peninsula and the Pembrokeshire coast.

3. Retrace your steps through the little gate to the ruined barn. Bear left to cross a grassy track and keep ahead beside a wall on the left. The path eventually descends and bears right above a

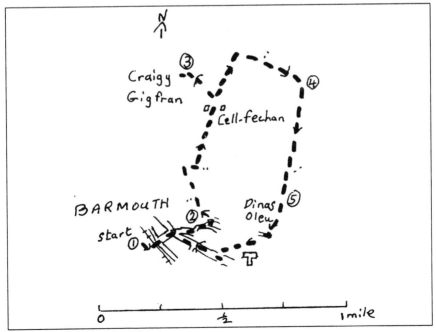

stream. Go through a gate and keep ahead. Ignore a small gate on the left. Continue with a fence nearby on the left, soon bearing right between outcrops then left again to a ladder stile.

4. Turn right and shortly after the track starts to descend steeply bear right on a path below rock slabs. Go through a tall gate in a wall and follow the path ahead to have magnificent views of the Mawddach estuary and Cader Idris range. The path goes through a gate in a crossing wall and bears left towards the Mawddach. Go downhill to a small gate in the wall on the right. Follow a path through gorse to a bench. Keep ahead beside a wall on the left and look for a small gate that gives access to the Frenchman's Grave.

The Frenchman was Auguste Guyard who lived in Barmouth during the 19th century. He lived in one of the thirteen cottages given by Fanny Talbot to John Ruskin, a socialist. Guyard had similar ideals and helped his neighbours by showing them how to cultivate herbs and vegetables. Mrs Talbot gave Dinas Oleu to the National Trust in 1885. It was the NT's first property.

5. Continue beside the wall and go through a gate onto the National Trust land of Dinas Oleu. Descend to a lane and bear left. Pass the NT's information board on the right and take a path going downhill between walls. Steps lead to the main road and emerge opposite the Crown Hotel. Turn left to The Old Tea-rooms, right to the starting point.

Barmouth bridge

23. Cregennen Lakes

Route: A lovely walk in one of the most beautiful areas of Snowdonia. The paths are mostly level, passing through moorland and a wooded river valley. During the walk there are fine views of the Cader Idris escarpment. The walk visits the two Cregennen lakes.

Distance: 5½ miles.

How to get there: Leave the A493 on a minor road signposted Cregennen Lakes (Llynnau Cregennen). Alternatively, from Dolgellau follow the A493 towards Tywyn until meeting a minor road signposted Cader Idris. Follow this road until there is a road on the right signed Cregennen Lakes.

Public Transport: Buses Dolgellau – Tywyn pass along the A493 and stop at Arthog, 2 miles from the start.

Start: Car park near the larger Cregennen lake.

Maps: Outdoor Leisure 23.

Nestling amidst wild moorland, the beautiful Cregennen lakes have been in the care of the National Trust since 1959. They were given by Major Wynne Jones in memory of his two sons who were killed during the Second World War.

The Tea Shop

In the wooded Gwynant valley, Tyn-y-Ceunant Farm provides a welcome halfway through the walk. Mrs Rees serves tea, coffee and home-made fruit cake. Janet Street Porter called here on her televised walk through Wales. Teas are served all year but if you are a large party or if it is very early or late in the year, it may be best to phone in advance. Tel: 01341 422300.

The Walk

1. From the car park turn left along the lane with the larger Cregennen lake on your right. In 250 metres the lane passes the end of the lake and rises to give a view of the Mawddach estuary. At this point leave the lane and bear right over open land to cross a ladder stile in a wall.

2. Ignore the path on the left which climbs to the hill fort of Pared y Cefn hir. Keep ahead on a clear path through heather to have the lake on your right. Beyond the end of the lake ignore the path on the right which has a green waymark. Continue with the hill on your left and reach a high wall on the right. The path follows the wall and crosses a boggy area. To your right there are fine views of the Craig-Las escarpment – the western outlier of Cader Idris. The path leaves the wall by climbing to reach another. Continue beside this wall and when it descends you will see a house, Tyn y Llidiart, across a field on the right. Go through a gate in the wall ahead.

3. Slant to the right downhill and in about 40 metres go through a gate opening in a wall. Bear left slanting downhill for 100 metres to another gap. Continue ahead and follow a broken wall on your right. The track becomes clearer and reaches a fork. Bear right to

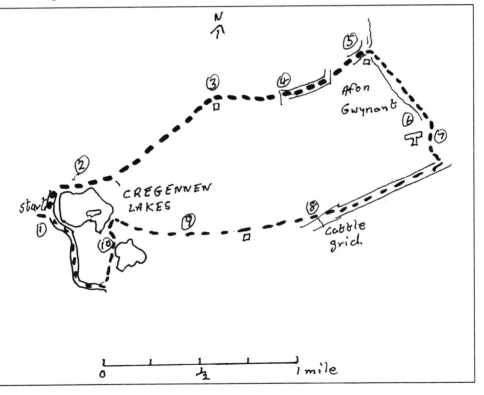

follow the track alongside oak and birch trees and reach a lane at an old bridge.

4. Turn left on this wooded lane with a stream below on the right. In 200 metres, at a ruin on the left, where there is a graveyard, bear right on a wide path descending through the wood. It becomes narrower and steeper before reaching a small gate at the corner of a wall. Turn right on the lane and, at a junction, bear right to pass in front of the Youth Hostel.

5. Cross a bridge over afon Gwynant and immediately bear right into a field which is used for camping. Walk through the field with the river on your right and keep ahead through trees to a kissing -gate. The path reaches a fence and curves left to a wooden gate. Turn right to enter a field and continue across the bottom of the field. Cross two small stone bridges close together and follow a wall on the right. Cader Idris can be seen ahead.

6. Keep ahead to descend beside gorse. Follow the river on your right and cross it when you reach a bridge. Follow the track uphill and in about 80 metres you will reach a track on the right which descends to Tyn y Ceunant Farm, your stop for refreshments.

7. To continue on the walk, return to the track and bear right to pass a barn. Keep ahead on the track through a field and follow a wall on the left to a gate near a building. Turn right on the lane and follow it for nearly a mile until you almost reach a cattle grid. About 30 metres before the grid turn right on a track for Nant y Gwyrddail Farm.

8. Go through the gate and follow the track as it bears to the left uphill. Pass some conifers and, just before farm buildings slant right to pass the buildings on your left. Cross a ladder stile in the wall and keep ahead on a track rising uphill. After crossing the next stile you will have a view of the larger Cregennen lake and its island. Keep ahead on a grassy track and, as it bears to the right, in another 40 metres look for a small pile of rocks on the left. At this point leave the track and bear left towards the lake and a National Trust waymark post.

9. Keeping the rocky side of the hill on your left descend the hill to another post. Walk in the direction of the lake, passing through a

boggy section, to reach another post in about 10 metres. Bear left towards a high wall – there are another couple of posts to guide you – and cross a ladder stile. Follow a path through heather towards the larger lake and reach a stream. Do not cross the stream but bear left to have the lake nearby on you right. Cross a stile and go through a gap in a wall. Turn left to reach the smaller of the Cregennen lakes.

10. Bear right and cross a ladder stile near the boathouse. Keep ahead with the lake on your left but ignore the small stile near the lake to have a fence on your left. Continue uphill parallel to a wall. When you reach the lane turn right. In about 50 metres you will see a standing stone on your right. Continue on the lane, which takes you to the larger Cregennen lake and the starting point at the car park.

The larger Cregennen Lake, below Pared y Cefn Hir

24. Dinas Mawddwy

Route: Field paths and quiet lanes explore this mysterious corner of Snowdonia. Arthur's last battlefield and an ancient church are two of the features on this walk. The route is not strenuous although there are several climbs.

Distance: 4½ miles.

How to get there: Dinas Mawddwy is on the A470 south-east of Dolgellau, at the southern end of the village.

Public Transport: Infrequent buses from Dolgellau.

Start: Car park at Meirion Mill.

Maps: Outdoor Leisure 23.

The woollen mill and coffee shop are located in the old station yard of the Mawddwy Railway. The railway line ran from Cemmaes Road to Dinas Mawddwy from 1868 to 1951. Do not miss the old pack-horse bridge opposite the coffee shop. Known as Pont Minllyn, the double arched bridge crossing afon Dyfi was built during the 17th century.

The Tea Shop

The Old Station Coffee Shop at Meirion Mill used to be the station master's house and booking office. The mill shop is nearby. Food is home-made and the menu includes delicious pizzas, salads and cakes. Open early March to the end of November 9.30am to 4.30pm.

The Walk

1. Walk towards the exit of the car park soon bearing left to cross the lawn between the children's playground and the coffee shop. From the left corner a path goes uphill to a stile. Turn left in the field and follow the edge of the trees. Take a path between rhododendrons and gorse to reach a stile and lane.

2. Turn left and pass a long building on your right. Pass some conifers and cottages on the right and after the last house turn right through a field gate. Pass buildings on your left and follow the

The coffee shop at Meirion Mill

right boundary of the field through two more gates. Keep ahead about 30 metres then bear left on a track that crosses a stream and goes through a gate. Follow a fence on the left. The field is known as Maes y Camlam. It is said that on these slopes King Arthur fought his last battle with his nephew Mordred.

3. Keep ahead on a wide path with fine views over the Dyfi Valley. Cross a stile into another field and keep ahead to a track that bears right to a gate and ladder stile. Cross a stream and follow the track to a fork. Bear left through woodland and keep ahead at a clearing. Go through a gate to pass above a house and bear left to a gate and lane.

4. Turn left downhill and, in 120 metres, turn right to cross Pont Mallwyd over afon Dyfi. Follow the lane uphill to a roundabout at the village of Mallwyd. Cross to the Brigands Inn. Turn right for about 200 metres if you wish to visit the church. It is usually open.

George Borrow stayed at the Brigands Inn after passing through Dinas Mawddwy in the mid 19th century. The Brigands were the red-haired bandits of Mawddwy who terrorised travellers for centuries during the Middle Ages.

The blue colour of the pool is caused by light reflected from the surrounding cliffs. The quarry closed in 1915.

3. Retrace your steps to the lane and turn right. Pass Pant Einion Hall on the left and stay on the lane as it bears left. Before reaching houses turn right through a gate and continue on a track. Go through a kissing-gate and walk uphill. When the track divides, take the lower track. At the next fork bear left and walk above a quarry road to reach a ladder stile.

4. Continue with a fence on the left. The path is bordered by a variety of wild flowers in spring and early summer. Ignore a Tir Cymen link path on the right. Descend with a wall on the left to another stile. Continue on the left-hand path and keep ahead downhill over two more stiles. Cross a track to another footpath and go through a kissing-gate at some steps. Follow a steep path downhill to a fence. Keep the fence on your left and continue downhill to a ladder stile. Walk down the field to an access road and turn left. In 30 metres, at a footpath signpost, cross to a small gate and keep ahead on a path to the A493. Cross the road with care and turn left. Bear right on a lane signposted Morfa Mawddach. In 300 metres turn right on a footpath.

This is the Arthog Bog nature reserve, an area of alder and willow scrubland where warblers breed. Orchids, marsh cinquefoil and irises grow in the meadow.

5. In approximately 280 metres go left on a clear path to reach the trackbed of the former Ruabon -Barmouth railway line. Turn right for 600 metres.

The line ran for only 100 years after opening in the mid 19th century. It can now be walked as far as Dolgellau.

6. Turn left through a small gate and follow a clear raised path with a fence and woodland on the left. Ignore a footpath on the right and go through the gate ahead to reach a track. Turn left above afon Mawddach with fine views towards Barmouth Bridge. At a fork bear left and in 50 metres turn right to pass behind houses. On reaching the estuary again keep left to follow an obvious path below the rocky hill Fegla Fawr. Keep the hill on your left to continue on the track as it leaves the estuary. Cross an embankment

and keep ahead to a barrier at another embankment. Turn right here to meet a path that runs alongside the Cambrian Coast Railway line.

7. Turn left and at the entrance to Morfa Mawddach Station platform bear right through a small gate and – with care – cross the line to a stile. Follow the path as it bears left along an embankment. There are superb views across the estuary towards Barmouth. Continue along the embankment crossing a number of stiles until you reach a road. Turn left alongside the Fairbourne miniature railway.

Originally a horse-drawn tramway, the line was built in the 19th century by the flour miller Mr McDougall.

8. Continue alongside the line as it turns left to Fairbourne and the start of the walk.

The Mawddach estuary

26. Llanegryn

Route: Ascending paths beside a stream lead to a green track which rises gradually to wild moorland. The descent is along a quiet access lane.

Distance: 4¾ miles.

How to get there: From Tywyn follow the A493 for 4 miles to the turn-off for Llanegryn.

Public Transport: Llanegryn is on the Tywyn – Dolgellau bus route.

Start: Lay-by on the A493 at the entrance to Llanegryn village. Visitors to the tea room can park in Cefn Coch grounds.

Maps: Outdoor Leisure 23.

Tea Shop

Cefn Coch Tea Room offers home-made light refreshments and home baking which can be enjoyed either in the dining room or in the garden. A former coaching inn, Cefn Coch is also a guesthouse. The tea room is open at Easter and the following weekends until May. From early May until mid September it is open every day (except Wednesdays) 11am to 4pm. Tel: 01654 712193.

The Walk

1. From the lay-by turn left on the road for Llanegryn village and in 20 metres bear left to pass Cefn Coch Tea Room on your left. Follow the lane as it rises gently and then descends to a stream Turn left over a ladder stile.

2. Keep ahead and, just before the entrance to a field, turn right on a path. Go ahead through trees with a stream nearby on the right. The path rises above the stream and continues above it. At a level area go ahead with an old wall and hedge on the left. Llanegryn Church comes into view across the valley. Keep ahead and cross a stile at some trees. In 30 metres, cross a footbridge and ladder stile on the right. Walk uphill towards the church. Keep the churchyard wall on your left and climb steps in wall to enter the churchyard.

The main feature of this simple 13ᵗʰ century church is the very beautiful medieval rood loft and screen which, according to tradition, came here from Cymer Abbey, near Dolgellau, at the time of the Dissolution of the Monasteries. It is though the screen was carried by the monks overnight through the mountains. The font is probably Norman.

Llanegryn church

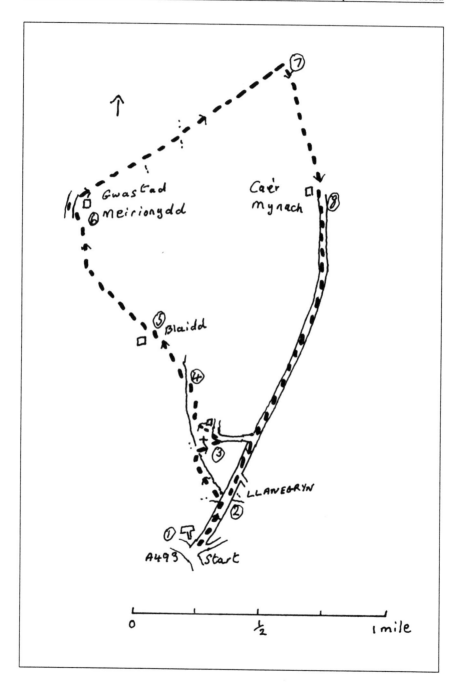

3. Leave the churchyard through the lychgate. Bear left and in about 80 metres turn left between farm buildings and a house. Keep ahead through gates to pass buildings and, just before the end of the wall on the left, turn right through a gate. Stay above the valley to follow a fence on the right. After passing a broken wall, which descends on the left, slant downhill to a footbridge and stile.

4. Bear right to have the stream on your right. Cross a stile and continue ahead to the next stile. Keep ahead over another stile and follow the right boundary of the field to a track near Blaidd farm. Cross the track and head uphill to a ladder stile on the left.

5. Walk uphill on a green enclosed track. Follow it for a mile to the barns and ruin of Gwastad Meirionnydd. Pass the barn on your left to go through a gate and bear left to a lane.

6. Turn right through a gate and then immediately bear right on a green track to pass the ruin now on your right. Follow this track and in half a mile ignore a ladder stile on your right. Go through a gate and ignore the stile on your left. Keep ahead on the track and follow telephone poles across the moorland. The track passes under the wires and reaches a fence on the left.

7. Turn right to follow a green track. In about 100 metres it reaches a fence and continues with the fence on the right. Go through a gate and descend an enclosed track with views to Broad Water near Tywyn and the coast line. Pass Cae'r Mynach Farm on your right and go through a gate to emerge on a lane.

8. Keep ahead to descend this quiet farm access lane. Ignore a right fork leading to the church. Continue to the next fork and turn right. Descend to cross the bridge in the valley and walk uphill to the tea room and starting point.

27. Aberdyfi

Route: A varied walk which starts by following the Dyfi Estuary then climbs to the ridge top lane above Happy Valley. There are superb views throughout most of the walk.

Distance: 4¾ miles.

How to get there: Aberdyfi is on the A493 south-west of Machynlleth.

Public Transport: Trains on the Machynlleth-Pwllheli line stop at Aberdyfi. Buses from Tywyn and Machynlleth.

Start: Car park on the sea front in Aberdyfi.

Maps: Outdoor Leisure 23.

Aberdyfi is an enchanting, small seaside resort at the mouth of the Dyfi Estuary. The village was made famous by Charles Dibden's song 'The Bells of Aberdovey'. The words refer to the submerged church bells of the legendary 'Cantre'r Gwaelod' in Cardigan Bay. According to this story the bay was flooded in the 6th century

Aberdyfi

because the drunken Seitheryn did not repair the protecting embankment. However, geologists date the flood about 2000AD. Nowadays Aberdyfi is a popular sailing centre but in the early 19th century there was a very different scene when the quay was busy with shipbuilding and trading.

The Tea Shop

The Old Coffee Shop is an attractive old building in New Street, just off the sea front. Toasted teacakes and delicious cream teas are on the menu. Open all year but check in the winter. 10am to 5pm. Closed on Mondays. Tel: 01654 767652.

The Walk

1. From the car park turn right. Pass the Tourist Information Centre on the right and continue along the sea front. Pass the library and keep ahead, passing Penhelig Arms Hotel on the left. Go under a railway bridge twice and shortly turn right through gates at a signpost for Roman Road and Picnic Island.

The Romans may have used this route to reach their military station along the Dyfi estuary at Pennal. Later travellers probably came this way as the road above was not built until the early 19th century.

2. Keep ahead and go through a kissing-gate to walk along a rock path. There are two 'escape routes' to the road above if the way should be impassable. Cross a couple of footbridges and go down and up steps. Eventually the path rises to run alongside the railway line and passes above a small cove before climbing to the headland called Picnic Island. Turn left to cross a footbridge over the railway and emerge on the A493. At high tide follow the road to this point.

3. Turn right for 80 metres to a footpath signpost on the left. Go uphill with a stream on the right and a fence on the left. The path bears right to cross a small footbridge. Go up steps and cross a ladder stile. Walk above houses and emerge on a drive. Turn right a few paces before turning left to pass a building. At the end of the building bear left and, in 15 metres, turn right on a footpath. Go through a row of pines to have fine views of the Dyfi Es-

tuary. Cross a track at a footpath signpost and keep ahead uphill.
Cross the side of the hill and descend slightly to take a path into
woodland. The path drops gradually and just before reaching a
wall it descends more steeply to a corner and ladder stile.

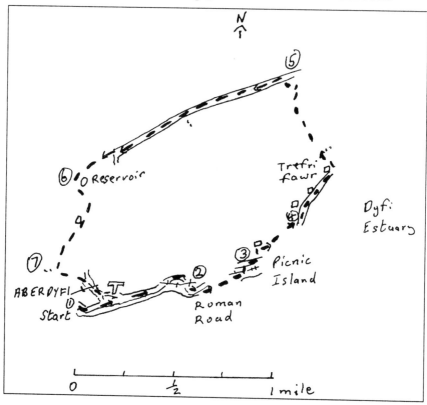

4. Turn left to pass a house called Sychnant and cross a cattle grid.
    Continue along the lane to go over another cattle grid. Pass Trefri
    fawr Farm. Behind the house bear left on a grassy path going up-
    hill. Cross a stile and keep ahead with a stream below on the
    right. The path becomes steeper and eventually follows a fence
    on the right to a ladder stile at a gate. Keep ahead beside a fence
    and on reaching a track coming from a gate, bear left to a lane.

5. Turn left to cross a cattle grid. The Victorian named Happy Val-
    ley is below on the right. Follow the lane over another cattle grid

to a junction. Turn left a few paces then bear right on a track. Pass behind a house and go through a gate onto an enclosed track.

6. On reaching a track junction turn left to pass a reservoir. Go through a gate and descend with fine views of the coast. Where the track bears left through a gate keep ahead on a footpath. Pass a barn on the left and cross a ladder stile. Keep ahead above a hedge on the left. Pass through gorse and, at a fork, go left. Keep ahead above houses to a low stile near bungalows.

7. Cross the road and pass bungalows on the left. When the road ends continue on a track. On reaching a gate take a path to the left of it and go down steps to another path. Turn left to a road. Bear right and go under a railway bridge. Look for a house on the right built by Anne Owen 1733. Reach a junction of roads. The Old Coffee Shop is ahead on the left. Continue to the sea front and turn right to the car park.

Tea Shop Walks - Spreading everywhere!

The Sigma Leisure Tea Shop Walks series already includes:

Cheshire

The Chilterns

The Cotswolds

The Lake District, Volume 1

The Lake District, Volume 2

Lancashire

Leicestershire & Rutland

North Devon

The Peak District

Shropshire

Snowdonia

South Devon

Staffordshire

Surrey & Sussex

Warwickshire

The Yorkshire Dales

Each book costs £6.95 and contains an average of 25 excellent walks.

In case of difficulty, or for a free catalogue, please contact:
SIGMA LEISURE, 1 SOUTH OAK LANE, WILMSLOW, CHESHIRE SK9 6AR.
Phone: 01625-531035
Fax: 01625-536800.
E-mail: info@sigmapress..co.uk
Web site:
http//www.sigmapress.co.uk
VISA and MASTERCARD welcome